The World Is a Book, Indeed

THE WORLD IS
A BOOK, INDEED

writing, reading, and traveling

PETER LaSALLE

LOUISIANA STATE UNIVERSITY PRESS

BATON ROUGE

Published by Louisiana State University Press
www.lsupress.org

LSU Press Paperback Original

Designer: Barbara Neely Bourgoyne
Typeface: Whitman

Cover image: *Rue piétonne centre ville Marseille Vieux Port—Paysage urbain,* by Mike Fouque.

The writing here has appeared, sometimes in different form, in *Africa Today, America Magazine, Antioch Review, The Best American Travel Writing 2014* (Houghton Mifflin, edited by Paul Theroux), *Hunger Mountain Magazine, The Literary Review, Michigan Quarterly Review, Missouri Review, New England Review, Notre Dame Review, The Progressive, Southern Review, The Texas Book Two: More Profiles, History, and Reminiscences of the University* (University of Texas Press, edited by David Dettmer), *The Texas Observer,* and *William and Mary Review.* The author is grateful to the editors of these publications and also for the support of the Susan Taylor McDaniel Regents Professorship in Creative Writing at the University of Texas at Austin.

Interior photos: Staircase at Gare de l'Est in Paris, Wikimedia Commons. Borges with Grad Students, Benson Latin American Collection, LLILAS Benson Latin American Studies and Collections, The University of Texas at Austin.

Cataloging-in-Publication Data are available from the Library of Congress.

ISBN 978-0-8071-7396-1 (pbk.: alk. paper) — ISBN 978-0-8071-7424-1 (pdf) — ISBN 978-0-8071-7425-8 (epub)

For the people in so many other places
who have welcomed me, a traveler

The world is a book, and those who
do not travel read only a page.

—ST. AUGUSTINE

Contents

The World Is a Book, Indeed

Reading and Blizzards

THE WAY I READ the book that remains for me Gabriel García Márquez's masterpiece, *The Autumn of the Patriarch*, was odd enough.

Maybe a bit criminal, too. And I'll get to that.

I was back in Boston. I was on semester break during a one-year job as a visiting assistant professor of creative writing at a brand-new campus smack on the orange, prickly-pear-dotted sands of West Texas, almost at the New Mexico border. To be honest, I might have been as surprised as anybody when, close to terminally unemployed, I answered an ad and they hired me on the basis of just a few short stories published in quarterlies then—but I wasn't complaining. I thoroughly appreciated the very warm weather under the huge Texas sky all that fall. Nevertheless, it somehow felt good to be in New England again, where I was from.

The temperature couldn't have been much above a dozen degrees when I landed at Logan at night, and a major snowstorm was reportedly on the way. I was soon set up in a great little apartment on Beacon Hill. It was sort of a box-shaped turret with plenty of old greenhouse-style windows. Apparently, the whole thing had been built years before as an addition atop the roof of the apartment house proper, a rather staid red-brick edifice there on Lime Street with its flickering antique gas streetlamps; the neighborhood, story-book quaint, was a nest of similar stubby side streets and anything *but* West Texas. Off to spend Christmas with his girlfriend in London, a young stockbroker buddy of mine had generously insisted that I use his place while he was away.

It was 1976.

The next day, the radio talked more about the storm moving toward the city. I hooked up for lunch with pals from college over in Cambridge.

There was my old roommate who was in grad school for architecture now and a Radcliffe girl who had taken English courses with me at Harvard. (We always used to sit together in English 115, a required full year of Chaucer for undergrad lit majors—the course entailed in-class, line-by-line textual analysis, which the loopy old professor in a worn-thin Brooks suit managed to make fun, acting out in impromptu charades on the lecture hall's stage the derivations of various Middle English words and such.) But what proved to be most important was heading off to spend the rest of the afternoon at the Harvard Book Store in Harvard Square. A couple of years before, I'd met a guy my age at a summer writers' workshop who worked there, a fellow hopeful fiction writer. It was one of those deals where the two of us had so much in common in literary taste and aspiration that just talking about books together, right from the start, was special, something we both always looked forward to.

Back then, the Harvard Book Store—a pretty sizable operation and not to be confused with the university's store, the Coop—had the reputation of hiring a lot of young writers. I suppose there was talk that afternoon about my adventure of living in Texas for the year, but mostly the discussion turned to books and what we had read recently, what we wanted to read soon. Probably because it did employ so many aspiring writers, the management seemingly didn't mind how somebody like my friend spent well over an hour with me doing exactly that—talking in the aisles and goofing off, only occasionally making a token effort to shelve some volumes from a box or help a customer wandering around to find something. The big sooty MBTA buses outside on Massachusetts Avenue crept by in the cold; bundled-up people hurried this way and that along the sidewalk—and in the store we continued to talk.

At the display table for new fiction, my friend eventually was shoving a copy of a book into my grip, passing it to me with all the conviction of a quarterback making sure his fullback had the handoff, solid and secure. The hardbound book had a glossy dust jacket with a patterning of lush jungle ferns, green on green, and it was the long-awaited new novel by the dazzling Colombian, who hadn't quite yet won the Nobel Prize, but—as anybody who knew anything about literature realized—at some point certainly would.

"I just read it, and it knocked me out," my friend said. "Take it, man."

"What?"

With a job as a bona fide assistant professor or not, it was a given that I remained borderline broke, most of a very modest salary going to paying off bills and the like. I could buy paperbacks and secondhand fare, but hardbounds on my budget were usually beyond mere luxury; actually, I was most often solidly in the contingent of citizens who had gotten used to constantly rushing out to put a "hold" on a recent acquisition at the local library after reading a review. Or maybe I explained to my friend that I was traveling gym-bag light—I had to take the train down to Providence in a couple of days to see my parents for Christmas, then return to Boston to fly out of Logan, and the extra bulk of another book while traveling, especially a hardbound one, could be a problem. He didn't let me pass it back to him. Was he proposing I shoplift the thing?

"Take it," he repeated.

Bespectacled, portly in a scholarly way, he smiled.

And he said it was a prime perk of his employment and a main reason why he kept the job, so he could read all the latest stuff he wanted, on an unofficial borrowing basis; he assured me everybody did it at the store. He then went up to the front sales counter and got a bag, telling me—as I zipped up my bulky parka at the door, tucked in my looping scarf—to make sure, of course, I was careful with the book. I have to admit it felt somewhat strange (risky? illegal?) for me, a nonemployee, to be walking out with it like that, absolutely sans sales receipt.

The next day or so was more or less otherworldly.

The snow began falling just about the time I started on the novel back in the apartment on Beacon Hill late that afternoon. Dressed, I read stretched out on the made bed in the small oblong bedroom, which had rows of those drafty windows on a full three sides—still, it was altogether comfortable, the silver-painted steam-heat radiators clankingly doing their job well. The first flakes at the end of the gray day were large and fluttering, like moths, but before long they were finer, fell more steadily as the wind picked up; it swirled the accumulating white in boomerang patterns beyond the glass, out there on the flat tar rooftop of the few-story building that was cluttered with chimneys and vents, plus a couple of old plastic lawn chairs surely from the summer before. But for all intents and purposes that had nothing to do with where I was, because I was enjoying nearly an out-of-body experience. It's one of the obvious essential powers of fiction, the idea of which still never fails to spookily baffle me—how simple black ink marks on a white pulp page can magic-carpet you from wherever you think you are to wherever, while reading, you *really* are.

And I was even farther away than West Texas. Or, I wasn't even within the usually accepted parameters of time and space as I read, savoring every word of *The Autumn of the Patriarch*'s lush, lyrical language. The novel tells of the dictator who lives to an indefinite age, "somewhere between 107 and 232." His subjects become almost a Greek chorus, via the expert use of the first-person-plural "we" for narration; they view him in what might be considered a revelatory dream light, and for them the old man looms as an omnipresent and powerful father figure, mythical indeed. They also find him finally dead in his crumbling palace in the imaginary country that's an ultimate composite of all Latin American lands which once had dictatorships—though, in fact, he never seems to actually die (he tricks them with a double), as perhaps the very presence of any dictator never fully expires for anybody who has lived through the utter unreality of such a regime. The rich prose of the long, rhythmically flowing sentences, the command of startling metaphor a delight in itself—it was all superb.

I kept reading.

I must have gone through about seventy-five pages before tugging on my parka again, to go down the flights of stairs and out into the blanketed, and all but deserted, streets. I'd already discovered a little diner on Charles Street, a couple of blocks away. Sitting on a swivel stool at the formica counter, I had a late dinner of fried liver and onions, with lumpy mashed potatoes and stewed butternut squash on the side, everything piping hot and set on a thick crockery plate. I still remember the meal to this day, and it was perfect on the night of such a blizzard. However, other than that, as said, I remember little, except for heading right back to the warm apartment and returning immediately to the aging dictator's world. I maybe made some instant coffee, very careful not to spill anything on the book. I maybe stretched out on the bed some more, dressed, while the accumulation deepened and an occasional plow truck would take another growling pass through the street below, the wide blade sparking bright when nicking the pavement. I kept reading, surely looking at the snow all around me once in a while—man, was it *ever* coming down—then back to the page. If I didn't finish the book that night, before washing up in the tiny bathroom and then dozing off, I certainly did finish its few hundred pages the next morning, when at around ten the gray skies outside the windows lifted. By the time I closed the cover at noon, I was practically blinded by the sunshine suddenly glaring off so much white up there.

That novel was—and *is*—something else, all right.

■

In the last dozen or so years, I've been doing something.

Much older, needless to say, but continuing to pride myself on knowing how to travel supremely light, I pack a small bag and go off on my own for a couple of weeks to some place far away where a work of literature I love is set. I want to see if anything different happens while rereading "on the premises," so to speak. I've read Borges's stories in Buenos Aires, and Flaubert's meditation on ancient Carthage, *Salammbô*, in Tunisia, and those two towering examples of the 1920s surrealist novel—Louis Aragon's *Paris Peasant* and André Breton's *Nadja*—in Paris. And, believe me, it's fine to be with a book right in the setting of the literature itself, taking long walks to explore the specific locales of some of the scenes as well. But I don't think I've ever had a reading experience quite like that of reading *The Autumn of the Patriarch* in Boston that December.

The next afternoon, with a foot having fallen, the streets were plowed, the subway running. I returned the book to the Harvard Book Store and my literary buddy there, who carefully replaced it on the stack on the display table. I guess we exchanged enthusiasms. And I guess we talked about how this new novel, amazingly, could be even better than *One*

Hundred Years of Solitude, also laughed together about a rather funny fact concerning the masterful English translations of the author's work done by Gregory Rabassa—García Márquez himself apparently had once commented that, to be honest, he liked them a lot more than his own original Spanish versions! I caught the train down to Providence that evening, visited family for Christmas, and I flew back by Braniff a week later to what proved to be an unseasonably *hot* Midland-Odessa. There, oil-well pumps bobbed in the desert and I began the second semester of my visiting appointment, which consisted of both teaching the bright, eager Texas students in a couple of freewheeling writing seminars and playing a hell of lot of golf on the kind of infamous Lone Star public courses—rock-hard and bone-dry—where you're forewarned by attendants to always be careful of "rattlers." There was also my crazy dating of a girl with a Western twang whom I'd met a local nightspot that could definitely qualify as a honky-tonk—really pretty, she had an uncanny resemblance to the young Elvis Presley, a whole other story in itself.

After that first year-long visiting job, I found myself some years later returning to the state, not West Texas but Austin specifically, where I live and teach at the university here. And nowadays I still often think about—probably dream about—how the snow swirled around the rattling old windows on Lime Street during the storm, how the silver radiators kept clanking and happily hissing. And whenever I try to explain to somebody the feeling of being caught up in a book that, yes, can't be put down, I tell them about the time in Boston long ago, up in a little apartment on Beacon Hill. I go on about being there amid rooftops and surrounded by all that blowing snow and with a novel that was, in a way, "stolen" from a bookstore for a while, as the true secrets of literature are perhaps always stolen for a while, too.

Talk about backing into a more-than-perfect metaphor for what all good reading certainly is:

Such a wondrous blizzard of words.

—Hunger Mountain Magazine, 2009

Au Train de Vie

That Voice You Hear When Traveling

I accepted with no other conscious prejudice on my walk than that of avoiding the wider avenues or streets, the most obscure invitations of chance. However, a kind of familiar gravitation led me farther on, in the direction of a certain neighborhood, the names of which I have every desire to recall and which dictate reverence to my heart.

—Borges, "A New Refutation of Time"

I don't know who I dream I am.

—Pessoa, from a poem

I'LL BE HONEST. I had a couple of large sadnesses to confront that summer in Paris. So I suppose it wasn't surprising that it repeatedly happened.

You see, I often found myself at this one spot at the end of my meandering walks through the balmy, traffic-empty streets of the early evening. The walks were in an everyday pocket of the Grands Boulevards, toward Place de la République—the outdoor cafés along the boulevards crowded but not noisy, if that makes any sense, the puzzle-barked plane trees even greener and leafier than the last time you noticed, if that makes any sense, too, everything in almost too-clear focus amid the thick honey sunlight that does linger till nearly ten in July and August in Paris—and, yes, after an hour or so of rather aimless and surely comfortable walking, I usually seemed to end up there again. And the "there" I'm referring to meant climbing the odd serpentine stone steps behind the stately Gare de l'Est train station; it meant continuing on along that decidedly shabby dead-end street, Rue d'Alsace, which overlooks the vast, cluttered railway yards, to sit down again in one of the big cushiony seats—old and salvaged from maybe a French Pullman car, set out right on the cracked sidewalk—and order a simple syrupy black coffee at the café called, tellingly and in a way too appropriately, Au Train de Vie.

But even that doesn't get at it.

Or it isn't quite exact to say I repeatedly ended up there, because it was somehow beyond that. It was as if I had to go there, or more so, as if a voice was telling me to go there again because it was where I was *supposed* to be, where I, well, I *needed* to be right then and at that time of my own life in Paris.

And now, months later and back here in Austin, I've been thinking more about this—thinking *a lot* about it, in fact.

∎

I've been thinking of it and how it all reflects a feeling certainly metaphysical that many of us have experienced. And I realize it's something about which many writers I personally admire have had a good deal to say, not only that icon of French *flâneurs*, the surrealist Louis Aragon in his dreamily meditative volume *Le Paysan de Paris* (*Paris Peasant*), but also the indisputable master of the metaphysical itself, the Argentine wizard Borges, with the same sort of experience often happening to him as well, probed in a poem like "Street with a Pink Corner Store" or the haunting essay that confronts the phenomenon head-on and analyzes it fully, "A New Refutation of Time."

All of which I'll get to in a bit, but first maybe at least some filling-in is needed concerning my sadnesses that summer of 2011.

■

Truth of the matter is, I'd received from the University of Texas at Austin, where I teach creative writing, an appreciated grant to work on my writing. Such grants have often kept me going as a writer, specifically for a stretch of sustained fiction writing (much different from the academic research grant I had very early in my career when I all but pretended I was a scholar doing interviews with writers in Africa, to be discussed later in these pages); this time the project was to turn a short story of mine—from a literary magazine and set in Paris—into something longer. The work would have me spending the summer in Paris. I would do the writing there and also investigate in more detail the actual setting of the scenes in the narrative.

Having taught in Paris on exchange a few times over the years, I had a number of friends in the city, and they all contributed to my email-organized campaign that spring to check around for a rental for me. One friend—a guy who was a lot of fun, formerly my departmental chairman at one of the Paris universities where I'd taught and the leading Saul Bellow scholar in France, now retired from university teaching and always a quite dashing figure, married to a lovely opera singer—came up with a deal he jokingly pronounced I couldn't refuse. His wife's uncle had just refurbished a very large apartment that had been in the family for years, and this elderly "Oncle Robert"—living in Cannes now and seldom using the place—was willing to rent it out to an American writer in need and at what turned out to be a truly bargain price that could fit the modest budget of my grant. It was more than ideal, five stories up in a frilled, buff stone nineteenth-century edifice of the type that the controversial designer of the Grands Boulevards, Baron Haussmann, would have heartily endorsed and, now that I think of it, probably was directly responsible for when the area had first been redeveloped, actually an upscale address for a residence back then; overlooking the handsome Porte Saint-Martin ceremonial arch built by Louis XIV, it had a full four bedrooms. And best was that there was nothing whatsoever touristy about the location even in summer, when Paris can be overwhelmingly and often discouragingly touristy. Far from chic nowadays, the neighborhood was a fine combination of the ready-to-wear boutiques of the busy Sentier garment district and the epicenter of the city's sub-Saharan African community today, working-class and colorful and alive, offering a concentration of cubbyhole hairdressing salons for wonderfully complicated African coiffures that I suspect has to be denser than anywhere else on known earth. The first sadness came after my teenage nephew visited for a week.

Of course, this shouldn't have entailed a sadness. And with me a bachelor and used to having lived on my own for so long, it's always been good to have somebody around for a while, especially a kid like my nephew.

We got along more like buddies than anything else, my assuming in the relationship the standard crazy-uncle role, I'd say. For him I was the oddball writer who, maybe because I had spent a lifetime around campuses teaching, had never really grown up and seemed somebody often a little more tuned in on his interests than his good, understandably concerned (but oh-so-parental) mother and father who did, also understandably, dote on him, an only child.

Tall, polite, bright, with an easy smile and longish hair in the Beatles mode rather than the buzz-cut more favored by teenage guys today, he was captain of the hockey team at his prep school in Providence (mostly a bench warmer and no star, who got elected captain only because his teammates liked him, he admitted) and also a budding playwright (he was intent on expanding the aspiration that summer and was in the midst of taking a screenwriting course at Brown U., very excited about it). He jumped at the idea I had proposed of coming over to spend time with me and practice his French, and we managed to convince his parents to subsidize the trip as a year-too-early graduation present. During the day he would explore the city on his own, soon proud that with a little fold-up map and the stack of Métro tickets I gave him, he was gradually mastering the underground system.

The kind of adventures expected to befall a seventeen-year-old ensued in the course of his trying to cover all of what he'd decided were the big-time sights. At the Eiffel Tower he stood in the line for the elevator and met some kids from Australia, hooking up with them for all to make the ascent together. Finally as high up as you could go that day, the second observation level, they took turns taking pictures of each other with their cell-phone cameras in poses as if they were falling over the retaining rail and into the full, wide expanse of Paris itself spreading out hazily soft blue-and-green in the background; he assured me it would be great to post on his Facebook page and his friends back home would get a real kick out of it. At the Arc de Triomphe he witnessed a police raid on a crew of those ragged guys—boys, really, African and only his age—who sell souvenir junk at the tourist hot-spots, tiny keychain trinkets cheaply plated and the like, the boys adept at fleeing fast from the cops with the stuff they laid out on blankets to peddle without a license. In the slapstick scenario of the particular raid he witnessed, the same blankets became ready sacks to hastily wrap the trinkets in as the boys scattered in all directions across the traffic of l'Étoile. My nephew described how the burly cops in their military-serious uniforms—garrison caps low on the brow and combat boots—were left looking very stupid and standing in frustration with hands on their hips as the boys, running away, laughing, mocked them in what was surely a perpetual cat-and-mouse game. He said it was all wild, at first excited to tell me about the crazy episode, next admitting to me that he did feel somewhat bad because he had picked up one of the dropped little gold Eiffel Tower trinkets during the melee (he showed it to me, and I assured him he shouldn't have qualms, saying that I'd seen them offered at four for a euro, so it was no great loss to anybody); he then told me how he would definitely like to learn more about the boys and their lives. On another stay in Paris, while teaching at the university at Nanterre, I had dated a French woman who taught with me in the department, Études Anglo-Américaines, and also volunteered with programs for African émigrés, so I knew how the system worked from her explanations, the boys being practically indentured to whoever had brought them to France. I filled my nephew in the best I could, as he listened to every word of it, intrigued and also concerned about those boys.

"But don't worry about that souvenir, man," I assured him again, "it's pretty much worthless."

Later at night, he usually headed over to the Kentucky Fried Chicken, a cavernous, weirdly illuminated place on Boulevard de Strasbourg emanating its greasy aroma for a couple of blocks in the bruised-blue evenings, now that it would finally be dark. There he would buy a Coke to entitle him to go to a table in a quiet corner of the first floor for an hour or two and use the free wi-fi provided, seeing as there was no connection at Oncle Robert's sprawling apartment. Still, no matter where he was off to while I wrote during the day or in the evening, for me his return was always the best part of his being in Paris that week or so. Such return involved some complication because the ancient intercom buzzer system had been disabled and all but ripped out temporarily in the recent refurbishing, an exposed spaghetti of wires beside the apartment's entry door and not yet replaced. That meant my nephew and I would have to arrange beforehand when I should expect him and look down to Rue Saint-Martin, an approximate time for him to show up in front of a tiny Japanese restaurant across the street. I would go to one of the long French windows, and we would exchange waves and smiles, then I would thump down the several flights of the spiral staircase—the small creaking elevator was slow, actually a rather dangerous affair—and unlatch the tall carved-wood door beyond the spacious *rez-de-chausée* lobby with its potted palmettos at the street. Sometimes I lost track of time altogether as I worked on my writing at the clicking keyboard of my laptop set atop a vanity dresser, tortoiseshell veneer, that became my impromptu desk in the pale-pink front bedroom, and then, checking my watch, realizing I was late and now going to the window in a bound—the apartment was too high for there to be any real vocal communication with the street below—I would see him patiently waiting, sitting down on the curb and contentedly watching the people and cars go by, smiling when he looked up and saw me again. I think I really liked how he would almost *materialize* there that way. After that we would sit around relaxing in the living room that could only be called vast (I once paced it off at forty feet), complete with a grand piano and elegant, if badly faded and worn, Oriental carpets. There would be a can of Stella Artois beer for me and a big bottle of fruit juice for him, plus for both of us the red-skin snack-peanuts the French love; the long row of French windows all open to the summer night, an occasional klaxon horn of an ambulance or gendarme squad car blaring loud, we'd talk more about what had happened to him during his day, laughing some in the course of it all, even discussing at length the screenplay he was working on for his summer-school class at Brown, the two of us bouncing back and forth ideas that he might blend into the plot and my soon getting as excited about it as he was.

Which meant that when he left, I drifted into a funk for a few days. I missed his company. The many rooms of the apartment seemed beyond empty, and then the predictable big doubts and questioning set in. You know, the usual sort of self-interrogation that perhaps many writers getting a bit older tend to conduct. And had I spent all too much of my own life sitting in a room alone and conjuring up in my fiction—with an endless flow of words and words and more words still—merely some phantom life, not real in the least and as incorporeal as the moonlight on the complicated slate mansard rooftops sprouting their ancient chimney pots I'd often stare at outside the apartment in Paris on those summer nights? It all brought up memories of past girlfriends I probably should have married along the way, starting a family of my own, that kind of dangerous thinking.

And more than once after writing all day, alone, I took long walks in the evening. And more than once I found myself there again, above the steps by the Gare de l'Est and at that café, Au Train de Vie.

∎

The second large sadness was, of course, much more pronounced and certainly larger and heavier, if sadness itself can be quantitative, measured as a matter of sheer leaden emotional avoirdupois.

It just so happened that all that summer an old pal from Austin was in a hospital called Fernand-Widal in Paris, had been there for over a year, actually.

He was from Algeria, but with full dual citizenship in the United States. I had known him for a long time, part of an international clique of guys in Austin who first gravitated together due to common interests and especially political world outlook. I guess that I myself was somebody who seemed to fit in with the others, being from a land far from Texas—New England—and therefore also a foreigner in Texas to begin with, which qualified me for at least pseudo-international standing; in addition, there was my track record of having logged a lot of time incessantly traveling in other parts of the world—Africa, India, plenty of Latin America, both the Spanish-speaking countries and marvelously (the only word for a place like that) Brazil. He was a stockily rugged, happy-go-lucky guy, seemingly always grinning. He'd never used his petroleum engineering degree from the University of Texas but had found a good lifestyle in cooking at a restaurant, balanced with working some import-export business deals over the Net with his brother in Algiers. A bachelor himself, my friend dated with about the same amount of pleasantly comical success and failure as I—we often joked about it, dating at our age—and he was so athletically fit that, past fifty, he still played in a local soccer league and refused to own a car, walking and bicycling everywhere.

Then it happened. Simply and suddenly, he suffered a debilitating massive stroke, which led to a bleak succession of failures that if looked at in any detail, or illustrative frankness, would sway the opinion, I suspect, of even the staunchest, most stingy-hearted Tea Partier robotically moaning about the alleged evils of American health care reform. After time in the ICU of Austin's municipal hospital, where he wasn't given the immediate physical therapy he needed because he lacked medical insurance, it only turned worse. My friend was moved to a supposedly state-accredited nursing home on an empty rural road out in the dry blond flatland peppered with scrub mesquite and prickly pear just beyond the city limits. It was a setup that looked like an abandoned and pathetically lost motel in the middle of that sun-baked nowhere, a packed-to-the-limit place surrounded by bleak chain-link fence, and within—and despite the best efforts of the friendly yet overworked staff—about as clean as, and smelling much like, the restroom of an interstate bus station; confused, disoriented patients in foam-rubber slippers and untied hospital johnnies wandered aimlessly in the linoleum corridors, and frightening moans of the bedridden could be heard from the open doors of some rooms as you passed. Honestly. It didn't take long to realize that the patients were just being warehoused, the modus operandi of Texas's inept state-run Medicaid program, among the stingiest in the nation according to published figures. When my friend's sister and her husband—originally from Algiers and now living in France—showed up to bring him to Paris according to a long-standing treaty that existed between Algeria and its one-time colonizer, France, allowing an Algerian citizen to get medical assistance in France if the variety of specific treatment needed wasn't available in Algeria, it was their first time in America; both of them were amazed, if not silently appalled, that this was actually the *United States*, that something like the nursing home was, in fact, to be found in a nation seen as so powerful and prosperous.

And so in Paris I'd go in the afternoon to visit him a couple of times a week at l'Hôpital Fernand-Widal. It was an old yet entirely immaculate operation, smallish and constructed in 1858, according to the plaque out front. Fernand-Widal catered to special services, including the kind of long-term rehab my friend needed, and it was located up toward Montmartre and in a busy *quartier* of Paris that was as vividly Indian as my own neighborhood was vividly African. I'd pass the receptionist in his casual blazer sitting at the hospital's little check-in desk—he'd gotten to recognize me and simply waved me along—and then go first through the outer courtyard, mostly parking, and then through the rear courtyard—some crisscrossing gravel walks and a long central arcade of box-cut lime trees, park-like—where I'd enter the quiet building and head up the stairs to "Secteur Bleu" and my friend's room, 104. I'd usually find him alone there and set up in a chair, often dozing off with the TV flickering on a news station; my friend had always been a news junkie, better-versed than probably anybody I'd ever known on the political situation of just about every country around the world. At the door, I'd maybe say his name, and he would wake with a smile as I entered the room, painted a fresh light blue and the same hue of everything else in Secteur Bleu, with the hospital gown and the crisp sheets on the neatly made bed all a matching light blue, too. Even if his speech was severely marred by the stroke, his dark eyes would widen, he would say only one word, breathy in his condition but the grin—showing two missing teeth pulled during his hospitalization—wider than ever:

"*Pete.*"

Some French alternated with some English as I sat on the bed's edge and we talked. There was his filling me in on my questions about his condition: if he was getting nourishment (he had lost the ability to swallow, was fed through a stomach tube); and how he was being treated (the wife of a French writer acquaintance of mine was a nurse, and she told me that l'Hôpital Fernand-Widal was top-notch, with my Algerian friend himself now assuring me that the nurses were good, the doctor who was in charge of his case was especially good—also, several of the staff were Algerian, so he felt very comfortable with them); and if his therapy was going well (unlike the warehousing of patients out in the bleak Texas flatland, here he was given a full morning of vigorous therapy every weekday, a real regimen where progress was monitored and assessed regularly). Yes, after the routine questions, everything slipped into casual, surprisingly mundane conversation. Talk concerning guys from our circle back in Austin, and always much talk about the upcoming election and Obama, whom he greatly admired. With such relaxed conversation, laughter, too, the whole idea of my friend being incapacitated could seem to me like nothing but a dream in itself that we both had inadvertently stumbled into. I mean, a couple of years before would I have foreseen anything like the scene of the two of us meeting in a hospital room in Paris like this, birds chirping in the lime trees outside the open window there in the courtyard where nurses wheeled patients this way and that to enjoy the afternoon sunshine, my friend writing words on a yellow legal pad when, as hard as we both tried to communicate, I sometimes couldn't understand the syllables he struggled to get out? And maybe as with a dream, I sometimes felt that all it would take would be a little jarring (hearing the phone in my bedroom ringing back where I *really* was, possibly, at home in Austin? or the sound of a growling truck clankingly emptying the dumpster below my apartment window when waking in the early morning back in Austin?), yes, something to jar me out of it all, this odd dream, with normalcy and life as it should be restored once more.

Some sadness, all right.

And that summer I thought about my friend so much. I continued to walk in the evening and, needless to add, ended up where I did go repeatedly, climbing the winding stone steps again to that place where I somehow definitely had to be, there behind the Gare de l'Est.

∎

Actually, maybe it's time now to turn to what I mentioned earlier, the writers who have offered their own input on what I'm trying to get at, this key idea of a voice calling you to a particular location, which probably often happens while traveling. And it seems I should address Borges first.

The essential book of Borges in English translation is certainly the popular miscellany of his work, *Labyrinths,* a paperback published in 1962 by New Directions and reprinted who knows how many times. If you thumb toward the latter pages of the book, you will come to, on page 217, what has always been for me Borges's most powerful essay. Titled, as said earlier, "A New Refutation of Time," it's presented as a two-part affair (a tricky configuration, with several textual reversals that in themselves challenge chronology), and in it, through dazzling verbal legerdemain, Borges examines many of those from the long string of philosophical idealists who questioned the very reality of the supposed reality of existence, all descended from dreamy-minded Father Plato (who begat Berkeley, who begat Hume, who begat Schopenhauer, etc.). Borges even includes a consideration of Twain's Huck, as he, Borges, shows how time and also space are not the geometric, rigidly enforced concepts we often too readily believe they are, recreating a scene from the Twain novel to reinforce how a strange and inexplicable feeling is possibly more befitting than any reasonable understanding of time and space being what actually defines experience:

During one of his nights on the Mississippi, Huckleberry Finn awakens; the raft, lost in partial darkness, continues downstream; it is perhaps a bit cold. Huckleberry Finn recognizes the soft indefatigable sound of the water; he negligently opens his eyes; he sees a vague number of stars, an indistinct line of trees; then, he sinks back into his immemorable sleep as into the dark waters.

With that reference and a pile of others, Borges eventually establishes the fragile nature of reality as we know it, just a glimpse of something fleeting and never clearly defined, there amid another more important psychic territory altogether. All the while, Borges is moving toward a detailed personal illustration of what he means. He describes how on an evening in 1928, while strolling in Buenos Aires, he found himself in a locale where he did seem to have gotten free of time and space as they are commonly accepted to be, had entered into that something larger, which, never being explained, possesses him with a quiet and true intimation of a state akin to maybe Huck's deeper sleep indeed. Listen to how Borges, again most beautifully, tells of it, a walk in the moonlight to the neighborhood of Baracas; it's an old and pleasantly leafy quarter of Buenos Aires (I once wandered around there myself) on the other side of the wide Plaza de Mayo esplanade and its aptly named and very pink presidential palace, the Casa Rosada:

> The evening had no destiny at all; since it was clear, I went out to take a walk and to recollect after dinner. I did not want to determine a route for my stroll; I tried to attain a maximum of probabilities in order not to fatigue my expectation with the necessary foresight of any one of them. I managed, to the imperfect degree of possibility, to do what is called walking at random; I accepted with no other conscious prejudice on my walk than that of avoiding the wider avenues or streets, the most obscure invitations of chance. However, a kind of familiar gravitation led me farther on, in the direction of certain neighborhoods, the names of which I have every desire to recall and which dictate reverence to my heart. I do not mean by this my own neighborhood, the precise surroundings of my childhood, but rather its still mysterious environs: an area I have possessed often in words but seldom in reality, immediate and at the same time mythical. . . . My progress brought me to a corner. I breathed in the night, in a most supreme holiday from thought. The view, not all that complex, seemed simplified by my tiredness. It was made unreal by its very typicality. The street was one of low houses and though its first meaning was one of poverty, its second was certainly one of contentment. It was humble and enchanting as anything could be. None of the houses dared open itself to the street; the fig tree darkened over the corner; the little arched doorways—higher than the walls—seemed wrought from the same infinite substance of the night.

And there he does find a certain sense of timelessness, unexplained because, again, it can't be explained. Nevertheless, this state of mind is very true, even to the point of being what he calls a "feeling in death," not in any frightening way but instead in some serenely perceptive way, revelatory, with a personal deliverance beyond the trivialities of the mundane; it's as if his own everyday life, like that of Huck on the raft, has been fragile and illusory, a mere glimpse, until he finds himself easing out of it and delivered back into a realm of those deeper waters, returning at last into an ultimate essence, you might say.

The other writer I spoke of earlier, Louis Aragon, builds on this kind of experience and explores it in depth with two hundred pages of prob- ing meditation in his 1926 *Le Paysan de Paris*. For my own purposes here, *Le Paysan de Paris* might bring the argument into better focus, as it takes it back to the Paris that I myself have been thinking about. In fact, my time there that summer was spent mostly in the same part of the city that had provided a territory for considerable thoughtful exploration by the surrealists of the 1920s, including Aragon and also André Breton, the latter in what is today surely the best-known surrealist prose text of the period, *Nadja*; intensely autobiographical, Breton's novel has his protagonist, the author himself, repeatedly gravitating in his frequent long walks toward the Grands Boulevards and, more specifically (and a little spookily for me), to the very neighborhood where I was living: "Meanwhile, you can be sure of meeting me in Paris, of not spending more than three days without seeing me pass, toward the end of the afternoon, along the Boulevard de Bonne-Nouvelle between the *Matin* printing office and the Boulevard de Strasbourg."

Early on in *Le Paysan de Paris*, a thoroughly mesmerizing book, Aragon wonders if reality is but "a delirium of interpretation," and in the subse- quent chapters he sets out on his own mission of exploring the Grands Boulevards that also attract Breton, doing so with a concentration on his favorite of the old *passages* (ancient shopping arcades) in the area, the Passage de l'Opéra, which, with its roof of cast iron and milky glass filtering the midafternoon sunlight, exists in an almost subaqueous glow for him, suitably oneiric. He approaches the whole project as if wandering through some foreign land, taking in everything with height- ened perception at last, and in his repeated visits he responds to various enterprises housed within the mazelike and usually empty Passage de l'Opéra (a shop for ornate walking canes, another for trusses, a run-down café, even a "massage parlor" that appears to be only a ruse for outright hookerdom) with an awareness that declares transcendence is near, that he might eventually find himself at an exact place where it seems he was meant to be all along, perhaps has been all along, and valid insight almost beyond life—or better yet, an enhancement of life—is about to transpire; the impact of it all can render anything taken for granted in life suddenly in the category of the definitely mythic. Here's a borrowing from the original translation by Simon Watson Taylor that the brave little publisher Exact Change uses for its 2004 reprinting; Aragon's prose is appropriately lyrical as he begins to sense a primal Edenic quality to what he describes:

> It is you, metaphysical entity of places, who lull children to sleep, it is you who people their dreams. These shores of the unknown, sands shivering with anguish and anticipation, are fringed by the substance of our minds . . . [it was] this sensation of strangeness which filled me when I was still a creature of pure wonder, in a setting where I first became aware of the presence of a coherence for which I could not account but which sent its roots into my heart.

■

Lovely stuff, no?

And it echoes Borges's feeling in Baracas. And in a way, both writers with their own aimless walking are travelers, too, granting that it is foot travel they speak of and in their own cities. And aren't we all travelers in our dreams, wandering alone and solitary, constantly being drawn to a place where we *should* be, for the larger perception we *should* have, a voice often urging us on, as described? In my case the voice was nearly a distinct whispering heard as my own twenty-five-buck, black-and-white-nylon Reeboks shuffled over the sidewalks of Paris in the warm evenings of summer 2011, where despite all that sadness and also, and often, too much time on my hands in Paris to think about everything I had messed up in my life over the years, I did what I did.

I inevitably ended up *there* again.

It would happen on any one of those evenings. And just to look up between the rows of mansard-roof buildings, as Rue Saint-Martin became Rue du Faubourg Saint-Martin, was to see at the far-off top of the slope the imposing Gare de l'Est—bright white and showing new red awnings for its many repeated oblong windows flanking a massive fan-shaped window, airily delicate and practically as high as the building itself—which meant I knew again where I was going to, had my cue, so to speak. And I started up that slight hill of Rue du Faubourg Saint-Martin leading me to the place, heading that way.

Early evening in Paris.

■

Yes, early evening in Paris, and it's balmy summer, the daylight still remaining but softened.

■

A wide cobbled plaza with taxi stands spreads in front of station. Right beside it is a narrow street, Rue d'Alsace, which offers yet more taxi stands; there's a long line of doors to the station here, always open in summer, so you can look within to see all those people, shadowy and with the many destinations they have, moving across the polished terrazzo floor, almost like a glassy lake they're magically walking on, the news kiosks and coffee counters busy. A dim street, Rue d'Alsace is an odd one, too, in that it abruptly dead-ends—or in this case is interrupted—at a stairway with a double set of steep white stone steps that must date back to the mid-nineteenth century, when the station was built. The steps, with sculpted banister rails, ascend curvingly on each side of a *very* odd little platform enclave about halfway up of weeds and litter and an arched rusty iron door; that door looks more like an entryway to a burial vault than anything else, though it maybe actually gives access to some kind of functional tunnel, formerly used, as somebody once told me, for baggage transfer. The individual slabs of the steps are as worn as old bars of soap, and in the steep climb you start to feel it in your calves, agreeably so, while the stairway continues to take you higher, finally to another level, quite far above the station.

At the top, a true other world altogether suddenly opens up, because as the narrow Rue d'Alsace resumes again now on this higher level, you're not only well above Paris, it seems, but in a wide-open space so removed from everything else in the hubbub of the city that it can feel as if you aren't even in the City of Paris below.

There are ramshackle shops and cafés along one side of Rue d'Alsace, and on the other open side, across the street's sticky summer asphalt, is a low stone wall, graffiti-splattered, that looks out over the sizable expanse of the railway yards below, leading into the rear of the station, now deserted. The long platforms go on for probably a quarter mile, and the rails atop the rusted roadbed are as shiny as liquid mercury, the crisscrossing overhead wires for the electrified trains a complicated, uneven dark mesh; announcements from the station play on the speakers, soft and warbly at this distance, and the chime music repeating its little truncated song of a few notes—the trademark jingle in all Paris train stations to signal announcements—is even softer and more warbly, nice. Or it's all so nice, in fact, that it could be *rare,* because this is one of the infrequent places in the city where, without the clutter of trees or buildings, you are in a space open enough that the sky itself seems to dominate. And in Paris in July and August, that huge sky at the end of a summer day can go unheard-of shades of rich color, sometimes big incandescent clouds thrown into the panorama to render everything more striking still. Men in grimy clothes congregate in packs along the wall in the evening and drink tall cans of beer, talking low, laughing low, Indian or African and delivered at last, surely, from labor at the end of a long day.

Across from the wall, back on the other side of the street, the very first shop in the row of marginal enterprises—those shabby cafés, a couple of cramped Internet-and-overseas-phoning nooks, a tiny old hotel with nothing more for identification than the standard blue-on-white plastic HOTEL sign glowing—is a bookshop called Librairie La Balustrade, which is wonderful and strangely intriguing in itself. Its facade is painted a bright cream color, hopeful among the surrounding sooty buildings, with a small hand-scrawled card hung behind the glass on the front door giving the limited hours each week the shop is open; the books displayed in the windows are usually left-wing fare (ecology manifestos, political manifestos) or philosophical fare (anything from Kant clear through to Derrida) or mysteriously spiritual fare (meditation texts, narratives on the visionary), entirely intriguing. The bookshop seems suitable indeed for the mood of this particular enclave of Paris, while you can't help but jot down in a pocket notebook every time you go there the titles of one or two of the latest arrivals displayed; such titles make for nearly little prayers in themselves and are often metaphysical in intent, no doubt, sometimes directly so, to cause you to linger on the sidewalk and, well, ponder:

La Vie des Océans, de Leur Naissance à Leur Disparition
par Yves Lancelot

and,

Quand les Sciences Dialoguent avec la Métaphysique
par Pascal Charbonnat

Oh, the lives of oceans, their births and their deaths! And—oh, again— when the sciences do have their dreamy and extendedly spirited dialogues with the metaphysical!

The evening smells somehow sweetly of the summer warmth as cut by a remaining faint tinge of exhaust, despite what the Parisian authorities claim to be their cleaning up of the city's air—a good smell, nevertheless, because it *is* the smell of Paris and always pleasant.

And where it all gets strangest, and maybe perfect, is at that small café, the one I previously spoke of, a block beyond the bookshop and at the corner of Rue d'Alsace and Rue des Deux-Gares. Rue des Deux-Gares is a narrow street thick with more of the blue-on-white lit plastic signs saying HOTEL, and it leads at an angle to the nearby Gare du Nord, the other of the two railroad stations the street's name pays tribute to. In its own appellation, the café is also wholly fitting, because dull gold letters on the tattered red awning out front do announce it as "Au Train de Vie," meaning in this case not just the idiomatic French term for "lifestyle" but nothing less than—with a crisp pun when taken literally—"the train of life," all right. In some long-gone hope of rendering it right for the location, probably back in the '60s or '70s from the looks of it, somebody apparently decided to give this everyday working-class café/brasserie a thoroughly railroad motif. The doors at the corner remain open to the sidewalk, and yellowing lace half-curtains hung from tarnished brass rods in the row of streetside windows allow you to see above them and inside, past a grimy flower-print tile floor and to the bar, short, studded with a cluster of actual headlamps from a once-modern streamlined train, all clear or red glass concentric lenses and polished chrome; on a high shelf on the far wall, above framed black-and-white photos of diesel locomotives and *wagons-lits,* is an extensive collection of moth-eaten conductor's caps, side by side. The finishing touch, and surely most appreciated of all, is how the few tables for the dining area adjacent to the windows on the Rue des Deux-Gares side use as chairs for clientele those salvaged Pullman-car seats, the artifacts also previously mentioned and lumpily upholstered in mustard-yellow faux leather trimmed with blue piping, the armrests the same dark blue. And to make everything even more right, on the cracked sidewalk out front, instead of having the standard variety of café *terrasse* setup, small tables and chairs, they have arranged there—facing the low stone wall across the street and overlooking the open railway yards and with the huge, huge Paris sky beyond often igniting in such very unreal colors—more of the coach seats and wobbly low wooden tables set between them. Which means that in the early evening after so much walking, you *can* end up there, you *can* ease into one of the old oversize seats with the cushion springs bulging out in spots, you *can* sit down and order from the leathery-faced waiter—who doesn't wear any waiter's outfit and could be just another working-class guy doing this after a day on another job—a single strong black *café-express* for a euro and a half, as brought to you in a white demitasse rattling on a white saucer, the waiter taking a little time to rearrange the couple of sugar cubes on the side of the saucer along with the single spoon after he sets the coffee down for you, "Monsieur"; and before long you *can* simply relax there, for me that place where I had to be—almost comically named the "train of life," but, as emphasized, so appropriate for it, too—and take in the scene, enjoy the ride, if you will.

Or to put it another way, you do get on board again for a soothing and possibly transcendent silent excursion into the evening, as everything else seems to vanish, because remember Borges and Aragon and what happened to them when they found themselves in places where they needed to be, where a voice perhaps told them to go, also think of the general mindset of another city wanderer, the poet Pessoa, a validly mysterious quote from whom I attached to my writing here right at the start as an epigraph, which suggests the mood of this state as well; and in that seat, sipping the coffee, not even realizing how long it is you stay there, the many sadnesses you might have with you in the world seem to ease up, fall into proper perspective—like that of my friend paralyzed and perpetually watching *CNN Europe* in the l'Hôpital Fernand-Widal, or that regarding my nephew, whom I didn't know well enough, and due to some drifting apart in our family, I had (rather stupidly) let time pass without getting to know him better, a sweet kid, so special that he actually worried if he had done the right thing in picking up a worthless souvenir trinket when the ragged boys peddling them fled the cops— and there you are above it all, flying along, traveling under the wide sky on a Pullman-car seat outdoors in the balmy evening of the Tenth Arrondissement and at a café called—please don't laugh when I repeat it again—Au Train de Vie, entering into a calming state of mind deeper and more meaningful than life but still completely amazed at the whole very wonderful journey of it, life, too.

∎

So that is where I would go, where I had to be on those many summer evenings. And there I seemed to encounter my own moment of timelessness, and there I wasn't fully sure where I was, but I realized I was somewhere that made me more sure of where I was than any other place I knew (something like this had happened to me on other occasions while traveling, my returning, repeatedly and half somnambulistically, to a small whitewashed stone church on a high cliff beside the sparkling aqua ocean during a stay in Rio de Janeiro, also my returning again and again to get pleasantly lost in the maze of the old jewelry-market district of Hyderabad in India, with sacred cows grazing in the littered streets and the welcome full explosion of smells and color and noise that is any marketplace in India), and if maybe all of one's time on this planet does seem little more than an insubstantial dream, this experience offered transport into the something larger, going beyond the dream and clear into what could be a dream about the dream itself, free of the ties of reality at last and laced with calm and understanding beyond understanding—truer than true.

■

On my last evening in Paris, before I was to fly out the next day, I had everything packed up back at the apartment and the place carefully cleaned, which I hoped the owner, my friend the Saul Bellow scholar's elderly Oncle Robert, would approve of if he ever showed up from Cannes. That done, I went to Rue d'Alsace again, or just ended up there yet again.

I knew I had accomplished what I had to accomplish on the manuscript. I'd worked especially hard on it the past week or so, my overall performance ultimately not disappointing, I hoped, the taxpayers of the state of Texas, the people who funded my university and therefore my grant. I now sat outside at Au Train de Vie for close to an hour. I'm not sure that the sense of being beyond everything, almost in another, more significant realm entirely, quite set in on this final evening as I plunked a sugar cube into the coffee, stirred the rich black essence with the stubby spoon. And the sadness I experienced now was not in thinking about those troubling matters I had to face in Paris that summer, the large issues, because in truth most of that I had come to terms with the best I could; I did reach understanding. (My nephew, back in Rhode Island, wrote me excited emails about how great the trip had been for him, even said that he was tossing the original idea for the screenplay he'd been working on for his course and now was starting a completely different screenplay, less contrived, about a guy his age who plays prep school hockey, not very well, going to Paris to visit his screwy uncle and embarking on concocted adventures with some even screwier Australian kids; he wanted my input on the new scenario he'd come up with, saying that the most valuable thing anybody had ever told him about writing was exactly what I had said to him, emphasizing that he should write about what he knew; his thanking me in the emails made me feel good. The sister and brother-in-law of my friend in the hospital finally had everything approved and in order, so that he could, in fact, be moved from Paris to Nantes, where they lived, and visiting him for a final time at Fernand-Widal a couple of days before, with the bed sheets and the hospital gown he was wearing now both a pale yellow, despite the room being off the quiet, empty corridor of "Secteur Bleu," I entered to see him smiling in the sunshine pouring through that window he sat beside; he appeared nothing short of radiant amid so much yellow, telling me in his difficult speech, smiling more, how he looked forward to soon being near his relatives, who, as it now stood, got to take the train to visit him here in Paris only once a month; I think I was taken by his optimism in the course of such personal disaster, our parting handshake eventually exchanged with both of us knowing we most likely would never see each other again, but still, there would always be for me this show of his sheer winning outlook, or unmitigated bravery—and that, too, made me feel good.) No, the current sadness now was more mildly mundane, and it existed, predictably enough, in my realizing that I would miss this spot I had often come to. I'd really miss being in Paris as well, where I had spent much of my life over the last twenty-five years and where I had many close friends to talk with about literature—good, enlightening conversation and definitely much more of that sort of thing than I had with so-called academic colleagues at my supposed home in Texas (where, if truth be known, I simply had moved for a full-time job years before, and to me Texas never felt anywhere near being what one might call home). I had my Bic pen and pocket notebook with a red marbleized cover laid out on the wobbly table. In between sips and looking up to that huge sky again—travelers with roller luggage walking by now and then, heading to or coming from the Gare de l'Est—I jotted some notes about the details of the scene there on Rue d'Alsace, probably knowing already that I would be writing an essay like the one you're reading now (several days ago I was told in an email that the café, utterly funky and authentic when I had been there, has undergone some rather clinical, and unfortunate, extensive remodeling), and I guess that I was just feeling a little lost suddenly and also pretty tired, physically so.

I mean, I'd had only a few hours sleep the night before due to anxiousness, worry about getting the apartment cleaned and making sure I had taken care of everything I had to take care of in Paris (including a complicated session that day to close out a French checking account I'd kept for years), and I knew that even the walk back to Rue Saint-Martin would be somewhat of a chore at this stage, seeing as I had to be up early to get out to the airport the next morning.

Leaving the café, I nodded to the wiry guy in a faded polo shirt and jeans who was the waiter. He had come to expect me in the evening, I suppose, and he nodded back to me, "Monsieur," then I headed back down one side of the twin sets of winding steps beside the Gare de l'Est. I told myself that I shouldn't have lingered at the café as long as I had: there were still some last phone calls to make to French friends that evening, and it was already getting late, the sun having set. But then—weary, as said, also pressed for time—I remembered I had my trump card, and a literal card it was. You see, in Austin a young French woman who was there for the summer doing research at the university's rare books and manuscript library had lent me for the summer her card for those shared bicycles they have in Paris now. The system is called Vélib', a fabricated catchword more or less translating as, indeed, "bicycle freedom," and throughout the city there are long racks of the matching things, sturdy beige-colored three-speeds, each with a generator light and a copious chrome basket on the front handlebars, waiting there for anybody who does subscribe to pay the deposit initially required and then the nominal fee to get a rider's card good for the year; the young woman—a genuinely brilliant professor of modern British lit at her French university, somebody I always greatly enjoyed discussing books with—certainly had subscribed, and I'd been using the handy mode of transport often that summer.

■

In front of the Gare de l'Est, at that cobblestone plaza, was a full supply of Vélib' bicycles, the little lights of the repeated stubby stands for them in the long terminal rack lit to make an extended row of green dots—jewel-like, intensely glowing—in the evening, which was a deep Wedgwood blue now and almost dark.

I walked up to the rack, felt the tires on one bicycle that didn't quite feel solid, then felt the tires on another, just right. I swiped my electronic card across the button-sized green light at the low stand for the bicycle selected, to hear the buzz and clicking sound of the mechanism unlocking—I tugged the bike free. I put the card back in my wallet, slipped the wallet into the pocket of my black jeans, also pushed to the elbow the sleeves of the open-collar striped dress shirt I was wearing. I adjusted the saddle seat up a few notches for my height and swung my leg over it, squeezed the aluminum levers on the handle grips once or twice to test the brakes, too.

And then I got on and cruised back down the slope of Rue Faubourg du Saint-Martin, aiming right toward the Porte Saint-Martin arch and my apartment there, the old buildings flickering by, my knowing maybe more than ever that it probably wouldn't be long before I would again hear that voice you do hear when traveling, in some other place, at some other time—again I would come close to understanding that particular something, which is so big and important because it *is* well beyond simple comprehension.

The bicycle glided along; the generator headlamp shone bright in the warm August night, the wind was fresh against my face—the bicycle glided along some more.

Really nice.

—*The Missouri Review,* 2013; and
The Best American Travel Writing, 2014

THE WORLD IS A BOOK, INDEED

My New Literary Credo, via Hanoi

WELL, IT'S A SMALL corner bar in Hanoi's noisy Old Quarter on a sultry, bruised-blue early evening, June 2017, and I'm with two Vietnamese writers.

"We are socialists," Do Tien Thuy laughs, "people in Saigon are capitalists."

The three of us sit outside, all but squatting atop tiny red plastic stools on the sidewalk, and we are drinking very cold Vietnamese draft beer. The traffic of yet more of Vietnam's ubiquitous sputtering motorbikes is thick and slow-going at a blinking red jewel of a stoplight here.

In Vietnam for a couple of weeks to investigate the country's literature, I've lined up meetings with several writers, including Thuy.

He's a lanky guy, athletic, and he has brought along with him another writer, Nguyen The Hung, shorter, smiling, athletically fit himself to the point of being buff; like Thuy he laughs a lot. Both are forty-somethings and in the military. They give some explanation of their rank (more smiles), which I don't quite follow, but to see them dressed the way they are (jeans, sport shirts, worn athletic shoes) you might take them for simply a couple of happy-go-lucky coaches of a local soccer team. Together they are the editors of what I know is the very respected *Army Literature and Arts Magazine*, a prime outlet for the work of Vietnamese short story writers. Right from my first meeting them, when they arrived in the lobby of the supposedly modern, though already comfortably shabby, Hotel Crystal where I'm staying, a block away from the bar, they've treated me like we've known each other since high school, granting I'm older than these guys.

Thuy's English is better than Hung's, and both keep apologizing for their lack of the language. A bit embarrassed about such needless apologies, I try to convince them that I'm the one who should be apologizing, my not having *their* language in *their* country.

They talk about the foreign writers they like, or at least are familiar with. Anybody from Mark Twain (still a staple in much overseas education when it comes to American literature) to Günter Grass (a good war novelist who understandably would appeal to military men) to Murakami (he has a sizable share of the shelf space sewn up in bookstores throughout Vietnam, I've noticed). Thuy mentions Larry Heinemann, the American Vietnam War veteran whose fine novel about the war, *Paco's Story,* received the National Book Award in 1987; Thuy has met him in Hanoi, and apparently for a while Heinemann visited Vietnam frequently and became an avid student of the country's folklore. But more interesting for me is when I ask them about current Vietnamese writing, especially anything they can provide concerning Bao Ninh, author of *The Sorrow of War,* a 1990 novel documenting the horror of combat for a soldier in the North Vietnamese People's Army. The book is a rare artistic tour de force, innovative in form and language and powerful in emotion, somehow even validly Faulknerian. The two of them assure me, in absolute agreement and obvious sudden reverence, that I am right in my appreciation, and *The Sorrow of War* is unquestionably the masterpiece of their country's modern literature. Better, Thuy says he personally knows Bao Ninh (pen name of Hoang Au Phuong), having dealt as an editor of the magazine with him, and he gives me some information on the man himself. Bao Ninh lives modestly in Hanoi today, he says, and despite his being much celebrated abroad remains a likable and unassuming sort, albeit rather reclusive.

Or I think that's what he is telling me, because much is lost, I realize, in the language gap between us. However, when we finish with literary matters and just talk about anything and everything, I suppose, with more beers ordered by Thuy in the busy place (as repeatedly brought to us on a tray by a pretty, lipsticked young waitress in yellow shorts and summery floral-print aqua top, yet when I see her quick-rinsing the customers' used glasses in a large vinyl tub—set out on the sidewalk, sudsy—I do wonder if I might be in for unwelcome stomach complaints the next day), the conversation soon moves on to larger subjects. They tell me they both signed up for the army when young, in their teens; they agree they enjoy their job on the magazine and say that more important than that, they have become each other's best friend, are lucky to be working together. I ask questions about the war. Some phrases and catchwords in the conversation get repeated as they answer (terms like "B-52," the feared American aircraft that pummeled Hanoi with incessant bombing, and also the very name "McNamara," once the U.S. secretary of defense and one of Johnson's smug assistants who contributed to a dishonest policy that needlessly resulted in thousands dying on both sides, McNamara seemingly as much a villain as Johnson to Thuy and Hung and described by premier Vietnam War chronicler David Halberstam, I tell them, as "the biggest liar of the war"), and after a few beers everything turns more relaxed, simply casual fun.

"American tourists, guys, anyway, usually come to Vietnam only for two reasons," Thuy pronounces at one point, "beer and sex."

Which could be an apt observation, with Thuy next adding, jokingly and knowing I already have a good pilsner beer, golden, right before me at the moment and set down on another little red plastic stool that serves as our impromptu table:

"Ah, you have beer already, so you need woman now, yes?"

Thuy's dark bushy eyebrows raise slowly.

We laugh.

When they eventually walk me back to my hotel before zipping off together on a Honda motorbike, I'm already thinking it has been such a fine night, they are two good men.

The next morning in the hotel room, I check my email inbox on the cheesy little Walmart black plastic tablet with a keyboard I use for travel and see that Thuy has sent me a long email, a wonderful one, in fact, which hits me pretty deep.

In his email he apologizes again for his English, says again, too, it was so good to meet me. And realizing, maybe, that we got too caught up in the idle talk during the beer drinking, all the laughing and joking around, also that much was missed due to the language gap, he says he wishes to explain his life a little more and what he hopes to do with his writing, having already published two novels and a few books of short stories in Vietnam:

> After the meeting with you, I'm always in joy. Although we have little time, not enough for discussion, but I have received many useful things.

And later it goes on:

> I'm a military writer. I was born in 1970 in the Viet Nam war. I suffered a lot of consequences of this war. Some my uncles have died in this war. I grew up in hungers, lack of books for learning. 17 years old I joined the army, just time the new war between Viet Nam and China continues in the North border of my country. I have been trained for fighting, but luckily for me, this war finished. So I have a big chance: to go to college. I have pass the exam to be a student of Writing department—Ha Noi university of culture.

> Most my books are talking about young soldiers and young people, they were born in the countrysides. They have suffered a lot from poverty and illiteracy. In modern life in Viet Nam, they have a lot of difficulties to get a job to exist. I also write about the wounds of the wars in past, but little. I only used the past related with the present to build backgrounds for my characters act to highlight my ideas. I am particularly interested in the fate of the soldiers, both Vietnamese and American in Viet Nam war, how do they live now, what do they think about the past.

And then much further on, concluding with:

> The ideas are so much, but my talent is small. Hope I have something for life. That's my best desire.

Reading it there at the desk in my hotel room, showered and dressed, waiting to go downstairs to breakfast at the Hotel Crystal (always an appreciated spread of rich coffee, fresh French rolls, and a generous pile of sliced fresh tropical fruit), I realize that Thuy's email leaves me somewhat untethered, the honesty of it, and also the, well, nobility of it. Or nobility in the largest sense, all right, considering Thuy is obviously a committed socialist in his communist country, as he's announced to me. I take the little elevator down to the dining nook, still thinking about the email. Already I know that I will continue thinking about it a good deal after that, and then some.

∎

And writing this now, my summer in Vietnam well behind me and my having tried to create the best I could in the paragraphs above what happened there in Hanoi, I will say that I do continue to think about Thuy's email, more and more. I've even fished it out of my account a few times and read it over again.

I wonder when I last heard or read something from an American writer anywhere near the essential sentiment in Thuy's message, his belief in the power of literature to accomplish something genuinely meaningful in the world, a felt, selfless attestation to the value of both life and art, including the way the two are so often interwoven.

It's not news that in the U.S. we're inhabiting strange days when it comes to what passes for a contemporary literary scene. People aren't reading nearly as much lately—serious fiction, anyway—and perhaps more distracting in a time of rampant marketing hype the noise amplifies to the point that one wonders if anybody actually knows what is or isn't truly worthwhile anymore.

As with so much today, from sports to politics, ego seems to become a contributing element in the formula. Writers of all ages are longing for celebrity, heady fame, often basking in acting as if celebrities though they are by no means celebrities, histrionically giving readings to the half-empty rows of folding chairs in a local bookstore, also making sure to create a puffing personal site online celebrating their supposed accomplishments. Probably noisiest is the constant tweeting about themselves online, which is close to de rigueur, with humility the very last item on anybody's mind (cliché-ridden, announcing how "thrilled" or, cornier, "over the moon" a writer is about a good prepublication review, that sort of thing) . . . and . . . and . . . but why go on here with what admittedly can have the ring of an all-too-familiar complaint, nothing the least bit new to anybody, right? Except to say that for me it *is* worth emphasizing now and then how the importance of the actual quality of the work itself amid an often discouraging state of affairs is almost doomed to get increasingly lost, or totally ignored, in the course of it all. Marshall McLuhan's prescient warning of the medium being the message—substance mattering less and less—appears to have proven as uncannily true in literature as anywhere else.

On the other hand, to put that up against the email from an editor of the *Army Literature and Arts Magazine,* Do Tien Thuy, subsequently leads to the point I wish to make here, at long last—how I know without question that after encountering Thuy's email that I myself have a new literary credo to keep my spirits buoyed concerning my own writing of short stories and novels plus a college teaching job that entails trying to impart to others the importance of literature. And hopefully that means significant literature of the kind any of us were excited about when young and had such strong, sky-high standards, daring and even ground-breaking writing with compelling depth, not simply the predictable and readily marketable look-alike fare that provides easy entertainment to be just as easily forgotten, merely more fuel for the always hungry sales machine.

Yes, it's there in those couple of last lines in the telling email from Thuy, which to my way of thinking can define and fully renew one's belief in the whole sometimes wearying pursuit in a lifetime of writing.

I mean, the thought expressed is close to perfect, isn't it, worth repeating over and over like a mantra indeed, an admirably modest central belief to stick to? And every time I do repeat it I again seem to be right there on a morning of thick honey sunshine in wonderful Hanoi, the motorbikes beep-beeping away below the open window as I sit at the long dresser/desk in the Hotel Crystal, rather disoriented by what I read on my Walmart tablet's tiny lit screen, but soothed and thoroughly heartened as well:

The ideas are so much, but my talent is small. Hope I have something for life. That's my best desire.

—Michigan Quarterly Review, 2020

In Vietnam with
Bao Ninh's Masterpiece,
The Sorrow of War

THE SPRAWLING, WELL-STOCKED bookstore Fahasa is probably the largest in central Ho Chi Minh City. Part of a government-operated chain, it's located on a wide main boulevard leading down to the Saigon River; the female staff members seem almost chic in their matching pink *ao dais*, the long and silky traditional Vietnamese attire for women.

At the top of the aisle for fiction in English, you will see—on prominent display, side by side—two paperback volumes surely often requested by tourists.

Graham Greene's 1955 *The Quiet American* is all but a given.

The story of a naive young American undercover agent who goes sadly wrong in his idealism during Vietnam's war of independence from the French in the 1950s, the novel has long been held up as an uncannily prescient blueprint of how the United States would later become involved in its own tragic war in that country. A good deal has been written about *The Quiet American* over the years, along with two popular movie adaptations and lately even online sites and blog posts providing detailed guides to locations of scenes in the book—mostly set in Saigon, now officially Ho Chi Minh City—so aficionados can follow in the characters' footsteps, literary-pilgrimage style.

The novel beside it in the featured display, *The Sorrow of War* (1990) by Bao Ninh, is not as well known, but definitely has its following, both in Vietnam and—ever steadily building—abroad. It garnered high critical praise when it first came out in English translation in 1994, winning a major newspaper award in the U.K. that year. Since then, the book has gone on to regularly turn up on reading lists for college classes in the United States about the Vietnam War, and it received some fresh critical attention in the cultural study of the war *Nothing Ever Dies* by American writer Viet Thanh Nguyen, winner of the 2016 Pulitzer Prize in fiction for his novel (part satirical, part political) *The Sympathizer*.

■

The protagonist of *The Sorrow of War*, Kien, is from an educated family in Hanoi. He enters the North Vietnamese army as a patriotic young soldier during what is known in Vietnam as "The American War" and sees heavy combat, which takes an inevitable psychological toll. But almost worse for him, at one point he gets assigned to an MIA body-recovery unit with the grim task of searching for and identifying corpses.

Kien returns to Hanoi after the war in total disillusionment and loses himself in an aimless dead-end lifestyle. Drinking too much, wandering the city at night and getting into fights in cafés, he's plagued by how much of his life has been stolen from him by war, eleven years all told; he longs to hold onto at least some innocence in memories of life before the war in an idyllic peacetime Hanoi with his high school love, a beautiful piano-playing girl named Phuong. Eventually Kien holes up in a bleak apartment house, closed off from the outside world. He struggles to come to terms with his harrowing wartime experience by writing a novel about it, though over and over he frustratedly realizes—in an edgy postmodern way, effectively metafictional—that novelistic form itself never seems to be willing to accommodate the full weight of his subject's painful truth.

The Sorrow of War is not a polished novel according to traditional literary standards, and therein lies—quite fortunately, I'd say—much of its power. It emerges as a riveting, free-flowing narrative, always unpredictable, which accomplishes everything good fiction is supposed to (the characterizations of fellow soldiers as well as Kien's girlfriend Phuong, raped on a military train during the war, are strong, and the drama in the firefight scenes, such as one in the Saigon airport passenger lobby in the course of the communist forces' final victory drive in 1975, intense), while the book also completely ignores a long list of the usual confining rules. It jumps around in time and shifts person in the telling, occasionally launches into meandering tangents where the assumed barriers between reality and unreality begin to dissolve, nothing short of hallucinatory.

Bao Ninh no doubt knew his material, one of only ten out of five hundred from the so-called Glorious 27th Youth Brigade who survived the war, according to his U.K. publisher's notes. *The Sorrow of War* was originally sold in Hanoi as a mimeograph-printed edition under a different title. The novel's honesty about the North Vietnamese army, including desertion and military brutality, rendered it banned by the Communist Party authorities in Vietnam before it became a bestseller there, both legitimate and pirated copies abounding.

Today Bao Ninh—a pen name deriving from his ancestral village; real name Hoang Au Phuong—is sixty-six years old and reportedly an unassuming, somewhat reclusive sort who lives modestly in Hanoi (he offered commentary about his country's past in Ken Burns's exhaustive yet not always successful recent PBS series on the war, a project possibly marred by Burns's characteristic earnest oversentimentality, as critics noted); some say Bao Ninh has been hesitant in seeking publication for several later novel manuscripts because of continuing censorship. In any case, he's published relatively little other fiction, with *The Sorrow of War* probably falling into the category of the kind of performance that, due to a visceral essence allowing for charged, idiosyncratic expression, might firmly establish an author's lasting reputation on the basis of just one important book alone in a writing career, an undeniable tour de force (Malcolm Lowry's *Under the Volcano* comes to mind or Arundhati Roy's *The God of Small Things,* even *Moby-Dick,* for that matter).

∎

My own admiration for *The Sorrow of War* goes back over twenty years, when an excerpt from it appeared in an anthology, *The Other Side of Heaven* (1995), which came my way as a book review assignment for a magazine.

Edited by the novelist and Vietnam War veteran Wayne Karlin, the collection built on the very original idea of presenting fiction about the war from authors on both sides. There were short stories by the American writers to be expected, Larry Heinemann and Tim O'Brien among them, but what truly affected me were the offerings from the Vietnamese writers, like Nguyen Hui Thiep, Ngo Tu Lap, and especially Bao Ninh. The Vietnamese work often exhibited a shared sense of the war having been almost an otherworldly experience, ghostly, reflecting an underlying metaphysical element that perhaps stems from the Taoism and Buddhism of the country's religious life and culture (Pulitzer winner Viet Thanh Nguyen has added his own insightful interpretation of this ghostly aspect in his study *Nothing Ever Dies*); reading the anthology's cut from *The Sorrow of War* back then, itself given the haunting title "Wandering Souls," I found the ghostliness most evident of all and focused my review on it.

Here's where Kien is with the body recovery and identification squad; searching by a river in the Central Highlands, they discover the eerily interred remains in a clear-plastic, American-style body bag of a fallen North Vietnamese comrade still in uniform, the corpse perfectly preserved and as youthful and handsome as when alive:

> Then before their eyes the plastic bag discolored, whitening as though suddenly filled with smoke. The bag glowed and something seemed to escape from it, causing the bag to deflate. When the smoke cleared only a yellowish ash remained.

The men in the squad, stunned by what they've witnessed, fall to their knees beside that river, an automatic response, as they don't attempt to explain it and together just pray for the soldier's departing spirit.

I eventually tracked down the full novel in the library at the University of Texas, having reread it two or three times since then. And much of the fiction by those other Vietnamese writers in the anthology stuck with me, too, which now and then surprisingly happens when one receives a book simply as a routine review assignment. In the spring of 2017 I decided to immerse myself in Vietnamese literature in preparation for a summer trip to Vietnam for further investigation of the literary scene there. I also looked up Karlin's email address and contacted him to ask if he remembered my review of the anthology and tell him of my upcoming trip, and he and the Vietnamese writer/foreign diplomat Ho Anh Thai, whose novels Karlin has translated, generously put me in touch with some writers to meet with while in the country. Once there, one of the first things I asked each of them was how he as a Vietnamese writer felt about *The Sorrow of War*, and it seemed the first thing each told me—a good cross-section of authors and all in utter agreement, much to my satisfaction and confirming my own outsider's view—was that the book is indeed the masterpiece of their nation's modern literature.

I heard it in Hanoi from two writers in the military who work as editors of the *Army Literature and Arts Magazine*, Do Tien Thuy and Nguyen The Hung; we sat on low plastic stools outside at a corner bar one very hot June night drinking quite a bit of good, very cold Vietnamese draft beer, and they went on in their praise of the novel. I heard it in Ho Chi Minh City from the novelist Nguyen Mai Son, until recently the head of the country's only university press, and from Phan Trieu Hai, a widely published short story writer and accomplished member of Vietnam's younger postwar literary generation. Hai now lives in North Carolina, and in Vietnam with his family for a month-long summer visit and to sign the contract for a new book of stories, he showed up at my hotel on a motorbike one evening to take me—rather shakily straddling the back seat—on a quick tour of the some of the city's sights. The two of us ended up relaxing with coffee at an admittedly unlikely spot, the small outside terrace of a McDonald's next to the handsome rose-brick Catholic cathedral, which did prove a quiet place to talk about books and a lot else for a couple of hours—ranging from the way the government-sponsored Vietnamese national writers' union functions (and, sort of comically, sometimes doesn't function whatsoever) to my own expressed pride in not having freaked out on the back seat of the swerving Honda in thick city traffic—the conversation repeatedly returning to, of course, a discussion of the wonder of *The Sorrow of War*.

■

I mean, even now, flipping through the novel here at my desk as I write this (my British Vintage paperback edition that traveled with me throughout Vietnam is tattered), I'm struck once more by how apt and memorable just a single sentence or a paragraph or two in the book can be, page after page of usable quotes, often searing:

On page 44:

The future lied to us, there long ago in the past.

Or page 82, with Kien in the throes of writing the very novel the reader is reading:

He wrote, cruelly reviving the images of his comrades, of the mortal combat in the jungle that became the Screaming Souls, where his battalion had met its tragic end. He wrote with hands numbed by the cold, trembling with the fury of his endeavor, his lungs suffocating with cigarette smoke, his mouth dry and his breath foul, as all around him the men fought and fell, one by one, falling with loud painful screams, amidst loud, exploding shells, among thunderclaps from the rockets pouring down from the helicopter gunships.

One by one they fell in battle in that room, until the greatest hero of them all, a soldier who had stayed behind to harass the enemy's withdrawal, was blown into a small, tattered pile of humanity on the edge of a trench.

And page 90, where the book's lyrical English title turns up in the text, going on to define a recurring paradoxical theme throughout:

The sorrow of war inside a soldier's heart was in a strange way similar to the sorrow of love. It was a kind of nostalgia, like the immense sadness of the world at dusk.

THE WORLD IS A BOOK, INDEED

Then later, on the novel's penultimate page, 226, an uneasy, tentative message of healing begins to take shape when it turns out—in a resonatingly ghostly way, a mind jump worthy of Borges—that the character named Kien who has been telling the story is no longer the narrator and the manuscript is merely a pile of pages retrieved by a deaf-mute woman and given to another anonymous narrator, who takes over and here talks of any soldier's life:

> But we also shared a common sorrow, the immense sorrow of war. It was a sublime sorrow, more sublime than happiness and beyond suffering. It was thanks to our sorrow that we were able to escape the war, escape the continual killing and fighting. . . . It was also thanks to our mutual sorrow that we've been able to walk our respective roads again. Our lives may not be very happy, and they might well be sinful. But now we are living the most beautiful lives we could ever have hoped for, because it is a life in peace.

Yes, I could go on and on.

■

Actually, and to bring this all full circle, I might return to that display in the bookstore Fahasa in Ho Chi Minh City. The placement of Greene's novel alongside Bao Ninh's does appear to suggest something larger, however inadvertently.

In the literary criticism of some academics operating at the moment under the label of postcolonial studies—though certainly not among approving general readers—Greene has been charged with insensitivity in his novels and taken his hits, all right, judged via an approach that weighs a writer's worth chiefly in relationship to the many injustices perpetrated in the name of colonialism. Postcolonial criticism is without question valid and significant, but at times limiting, if not somewhat uninformed in this case, when one considers how upon publication in

1955, *The Quiet American* was often seen as—and more than once chastised for—being anti-Western and an indictment of colonialism itself (a jingoistic pro-American review, windy yet revealing, by the once-fashionable *New Yorker* critic A. J. Liebling a prime example); postcolonial criticism also tends to overlook the fact that Greene, a lifelong peripatetic traveler to offbeat spots, was known to have been an appreciated supporter of a number of writers from developing countries.

In truth, *The Quiet American* is an accurate reflection of the novel's own era and character viewpoint, just as *The Sorrow of War* stands as the same for its particular era and character viewpoint; both are vital documents that contribute to portraying the long arc of the trials of a small country whose people suffered through a near epically unsettled twentieth-century history. More important is that each book, in its own very different way, is an exceptional artistic achievement, moving and entirely beautifully written.

And maybe one final observation figures in here, too, how Greene had a track record of championing risky, unconventional works in the novel genre overall (Irish writer Flann O'Brien's *At Swim-Two-Birds;* Vladimir Nabokov's *Lolita*, which Greene put on his list of the three best books of the year when it was still being circulated underground by a small and shady French publisher of soft porn before major publication elsewhere, etc.). I've found no evidence that Greene ever gave any public comment on *The Sorrow of War,* and seeing as he died in 1991, shortly after the book's formal issuing in Vietnam, it's unlikely he did. Nevertheless, my guess is—or I definitely like to think, anyway—that with such admiration for the unconventional plus his other various predilections I mention, Greene might have deferred to Bao Ninh's book if he'd been asked for an opinion, acknowledging it as a novel perhaps solidly surpassing his own and having become, most deservedly so, what it has become today: as said, Vietnamese literature's modern masterpiece.

Believe me, *The Sorrow of War* is that good.

—*Notre Dame Review,* 2019

Driving in São Paulo at Night with a Good Friend Who Has Died

And on my soul hung the dull weight
Of some intolerable fate.
  —Abraham Cowley, seventeenth-century English poet

Death is the dark backing that a mirror needs if we are to see anything.
  —Saul Bellow

SATURDAY, AND I HAVE taken the Metrô to your modernistic home on the outskirts of São Paulo, May 2012, and now there is the fine meal of feijoada.

It's what your wife, gracious Marlene, has prepared, as served on good linen, and your two grown sons are there with their girlfriends and kids, including lanky fifteen-year-old João, nicknamed Johnny, who speaks fluent English and drills me with questions about basketball and the American NBA.

■

Everybody laughs a lot. I keep repeating how this might be the best feijoada I've ever had in my life. And I'm not kidding. Marlene's particular application of the Brazilian national dish of stewed meat and black beans atop heaped white rice has a very spicy tang, the slices of oranges on the side of the light green china there for aesthetic reasons if nothing else—nice. I tell the others maybe a story of the feijoada I have been eating in grimy working-class restaurants near the Hotel Itamarati in the old downtown of the city, Centro, which is where I've chosen to stay while giving lectures here at the university rather than booking into one of the new upscale hotels amid the cluster of skyscrapers in São Paulo that is chic Avenida Paulista.

Your sons both laugh some more about the kind of places I have been going to for meals, joke that I am a brave man, though I say that the stark downtown restaurant/snack bars are great, and you nod, agreeing that such is the real Brazil.

After the meal—a party of sorts, really, because it is Marlene's birthday—everybody else is watching a Saturday-night TV variety show in the spacious living room, so much tinted glass and a polished terra cotta floor, the low-slung, bone-white furniture. But we have left them and gone to your study, where a single lamp glows as we talk. We can vaguely hear the music from the show, and after we discuss my three lectures upcoming next week that you have arranged for me to come here to Brazil to deliver—Hemingway, Faulkner, and Fitzgerald as seen in their role as story writers by me, an American story writer, though one not fit to even wander lost in the shadow of those masters, needless to add—yes, after such more or less business talk we soon settle into larger literary conversation, the way we always settle into larger literary conversation. The walls of the study rise high with books, a library ladder needed to reach those up top, where you go now, saying you have something special to show me. And something definitely special it is.

I look at you smiling up there, in neat jeans, loafers, and a dark polo shirt with the collar open, still slim and somehow quite youthful at your age, prematurely gray hair cut short; you continue to smile, assuring me again I will *really* like to see what you have for me. You lift the book from the shelf, and I immediately recognize its cover, the iconic red, yellow, and black pattern of harlequin diamonds of what I almost can't believe is a 1922 first edition of Mário de Andrade's *Paulicéia desvairada*, which gets translated in English as *Hallucinated City*. (Of course, watching you carefully descending the several steps of the ladder, I have no way of telling you then what I do know now—that you will die within a year, that the diagnosis of pancreatic cancer will come so unexpectedly; and back in Austin where I live and teach, where I first met you, in fact, when you came as a faculty member for those few years, I will receive alarmed emails from our mutual friends in São Paulo updating me almost by the hour on your condition in the hospital, before your death just weeks after the diagnosis.) Indeed, you do want to show me the book, now that we have been excitedly talking about the poet Mário de Andrade—there's my current obsession with his work, even pronouncing that *Paulicéia desvairada* might reasonably be considered alongside another major document of modernism published in the same year, *The Waste Land*, no less—and after you pass the slim volume to me, my actually holding this extremely rare first edition seems an event, well, nearly sacred. I handle it gently, as one might a cooing dove; with the limited Portuguese I have—not all that much—I manage to find favorite moments in the book that is a sequence of linked poems about the author's visionary wanderings through his beloved city, São Paulo, lines from it that I already have close to memorized. Mário de Andrade was in his twenties when he wrote *Paulicéia desvairada*. He was a member of the iconoclastic group of young people from the groundbreaking Modern Art Week festival that took place in São Paulo in 1922—everybody from the expressionist painter Anita Malfatti to the composer Heitor Villa-Lobos to the sculptor Victor Brecheret, figures who in later life would go on to define Brazilian literary and arts culture in the twentieth century—and, in truth, to think of the wonder of this work being produced by somebody his age is startling on its own. I then read aloud some of those lines, what in English would be:

The winters of São Paulo are like the burial of virgins!

And:

São Paulo is one big stage for Russian ballets!

And:

My soul hunchbacked like Avenida São João,
And they say clowns are happy!
I never rattle the little bells in my harlequinate interior—
São Paulo, oh my beloved, there are weddings like that, like you, my city:
No one will ever attend them!

We marvel together at the grace of de Andrade's verse, the remarkable imagery and rolling rhythm. You explain to me that you bought the book when you were a grad student and just about totally broke many years ago, but you managed to borrow and scrape together the money, because you had to have that first edition. Which is when, slowly paging through the book again, I flip back and notice the inscription up front.

■

It is your handwriting, careful and precise in black fountain-pen ink on the slightly discolored page, and I can understand some of the Portuguese though not all; I pass the book back to you, ask you what it says. At first you are hesitant, looking somewhat embarrassed, but I insist.

■

Reluctantly, softly, you translate the long inscription for me, how it says that you know that by inscribing this book to your two sons, Ivan and João—who were just kids then, maybe eight and ten—you are seriously ruining its value, but in the inscription you say that you want them to have it in life, because, as it also says, what is any book if there is not love? I suspect it does embarrass you, while I wonder if I have ever seen a more lovely inscription, one that manages to say so much about the worth of any book only because it is what it should be, not a book but the stuff of the human heart and part of *life* itself. That throws me a bit, because it is so right.

Marlene knocks and comes in. She smiles, asking if we would like another coffee. I try to make a joke about how I, unlike any true Brazilian, am an unsophisticated and also always cautious American when it comes to caffeine. Actually, I know I am a nothing short of a confirmed amateur, and as good as the earthy, rich Brazilian espresso is, *cafezinho*, if I have another cup at this point I can all but forget my sleep back at the comfortable if small room at the Hotel Itamarati. The Itamarati is an older, probably once-grand place in Centro, but now merely everyday at best, even shabby. Yet I am maybe also thinking that the past couple of nights I have almost welcomed the gentle insomnia of travel, leaving the drapes open on the room's big French window overlooking the hodgepodge of red-tile roofs lower down. There's a view clear past several crumbling concrete high-rise apartment buildings of the type that characterize any older quarter in São Paulo and to the lumpy hills beyond, a buttery moon tacked up in the city sky the last few nights for a scene so perfect that I want to think that it isn't *at all* real; or, to put it another way, lying on the bed, looking at that moon, listening to the grumbling little hotel refrigerator kick in and out of gear, I feel that this whole business of my being here in São Paulo, thousands of miles away from everything else that has been my life so far—and in a place that also feels uncannily *familiar*—all could be half dreamt. Standing in the doorway before she leaves, Marlene says she understands, she knows that too much caffeine can be troublesome when one is not used to it, and she smiles again, nods; she quietly closes the door and lets us return to our conversation. (I wonder why, as I write this now, I use no actual dialogue, make no attempt to reproduce verbatim what we did say and what I do recall quite well. And I did present in translation here those lines from Mário de Andrade, the poetry we took turns reading aloud and translating in the yellow-lit, book-lined study, you at your free-form desk and me in a comfortable chrome-and-black-leather sling chair there that evening. However, already I see that I have given no direct lines from our conversation to create the exchanges, something that I as a fiction writer am used to doing, with many direct lines of dialogue presented in a short story or novel—the absence seems very strange.) I suppose I check the time, and while the Saturday has been so enjoyable, invited to spend time with your family like this, I tell you that maybe you should drop me off at the suburban Metrô station for me to catch a late train and get back to Centro and the Hotel Itamarati there.

But you will hear nothing of it. You say you will drive me into the city, door-to-door service to the Itamarati, you assure me.

And then an idea seems to come to you. You say that on this night of our good talk about Mário de Andrade, we shall, in fact, go see what had once been the home of Mário de Andrade in the city. You say we will drive around some, too, perhaps see other spots in sprawling São Paulo, itself overwhelmingly large enough that I know nobody is really sure of the population—twenty million? twenty-five?—because on a fine fall night in May it will be a perfect time to explore the city.

And to be honest, that's when it all starts.

Outside, the night air is crisp, and it is fully autumn on this side of the equator. I wait in the short driveway, looking at the woods of the dark hillside city park across the street, thinking again, maybe, of the marvel of actually holding a rare first edition of *Paulicéia desvairada* like that. The electric overhead garage door lifts in a stutter of squeaks, and you jerkily back out the black Volkswagen Golf, always having been a pretty bad driver; the brake lights blink like red jewels. Then I get in, for you to admit—in your pleasant yet sometimes rather scattered way, energetic and ever hopeful, too—that you are not entirely sure how to get to the so-named Casa de Mário de Andrade, now a designated historic landmark, apparently. Nevertheless, you explain that you have been there on a couple of occasions years ago, so you *think* you know how to find it—and I laugh. With the little VW weaving through the hilly, serpentine side streets of the well-groomed São Paulo suburbs, the traffic soon begins to build; closer to the city proper and the freeway, we encounter cars backed up at stoplights in these darkened neighborhoods of such stylish homes, because even if it is ten o'clock, people are heading into the city, where nightlife never gets into full swing until around midnight at the earliest, I know, especially on a Saturday. To finally be on the multilane freeway that rings the city is almost to be delivered into another understanding of travel altogether, and you accelerate onto the silky lanes, the engine building up to a steady hum and the orange speedometer needle settling high as we approach the glow of airy high-rises and skyscrapers, a veritable ongoing forest of them for São Paulo at night. We can see a new bridge over a river that is like a whimsical commentary on the idea of a suspension bridge, one of those deals where the cables resemble the spreading strings on a harp—shining, elongated silvery strands—and I say how beautiful it is.

The overhead signs for street exits flicker by; there is our talking and talking together some more, perhaps your eventually wondering aloud exactly which exit you should take for the Barra Funda district, the location of de Andrade's home. You point out the daring complex of wildly angled planes, domes, pillars, and arches—spot-lit, very white—that is an international cultural and exhibition center designed by Oscar Niemeyer, and as I've learned, the work of this world-renowned architect, who is still alive and residing in Rio de Janeiro at one hundred or more, is everywhere in São Paulo; in fact, the abundance of his work here can sometimes make it feel as if the entire city exists simply as a conglomerate and full-fledged architectural tribute to the man. We continue to speed along on the wide, smooth freeway, the taillights of the cars all around us leaving bleeding streaks in the black, and I launch into a couple of stories of my own about Niemeyer. I tell of how back in a semirural pocket of Rhode Island, where my first years were spent in our family's large old country house—supposedly built on the stone foundation of a barn from colonial times—my sister and I as kids would pore over those pictures in the big, early 1960s issues of *Life* magazine and find ourselves amazed at the marvel of Niemeyer's best-known project, Brasília, at the time a brand-new national capital, beyond futuristic and plunked down right on the high and vast interior plains; my sister would finally sigh in exasperation, there with the glossy magazine showing the mesmerizing color photos of ultramodern Brasília open on her lap: "Why can't *our* lives be like that!" And you laugh, and I guess that only prompts another story, about a mandatory seventh grade trip on a bumpy orange school bus down to New York City to visit the United Nations, housed in Niemeyer's building for its headquarters, Le Corbusier also contributing to the design; with its clean, strikingly bold lines, the celebrated structure made such a strong impression on me that I got my father to buy me a plastic model kit that was an exact replica of it to excitedly build. I stared at it for hours in my room once it was finished, and like my sister I myself often wondered there in ever-so-poky, hopelessly old-fashioned Rhode Island, "Why can't *our* lives be like that!" You laugh at that as well.

Suddenly you swerve, more absent-mindedly than recklessly, car horns blaring at us, though you do manage to move over to the inside lane and the turnoff you *think* is the right one for Rua Lopes Chaves and de Andrade's home.

Then you guiltily smile as we glide onto the empty, dangerously short exit ramp, tell me that maybe this *isn't* the right one for Rua Lopes Chaves and you should have waited until the *next* exit.

And with that I really laugh, even shake my head.

■

(One good thing about my couple of weeks in Brazil is that we have managed to more or less avoid what was the regrettable, but rather absurd, too, story of your own three years at the University of Texas. How you had left your position at Universidade de São Paulo to accept a job in Austin, recruited for a prestigious endowed full professorship in the Department of Spanish and Portuguese, and how, when a new chairperson took over, an associate professor with unimpressive credentials, she made it a first order of business—who knows why, except for possible academic envy—to tell you that your research was not in line with what she saw as the mission of the department, one that was lately a confused operation on campus, plagued by faculty arguments and resignations; falling in academic ranking, it seemed to be currently getting by on the remnants of its reputation from an earlier era, when it had been considered one of the very best in the country, decidedly elite. Back then, in the '60s and '70s, it attracted a long list of major writers from Latin America on visiting appointments—among them Borges himself, who actually taught regular course-credit classes in 1960–61—and the department also worked closely with the university press and its Pan American Literature Series, which published in translation, usually for the first time in the U.S., just about every important modern author from the region. And while it hurt you initially, such an unforeseen personal assault from the young chairperson, emphatically contained in her detailed two-page letter criticizing your performance in the department, it made you and Marlene re-evaluate the few years in Austin; quietly and with substantial dignity on your part, you resigned, deciding to return to the university in São Paulo, admittedly at a much lower salary. I know that I always seemed to be the one who was close to enraged by that sequence of events, triggered by an American academic passing judgment on somebody like you, author of the several thoroughly original books that had given you an undeniable international reputation; this new chairperson was somebody whose brief list of publications included—we could smile about this later—research on the topic of dildos in Hispanic writing (no exaggeration), as specifically targeted approaches such as gender/sexuality studies and politically oriented postcolonial studies had become the encouraged—sometimes ruling—way literature was to be studied in that department. Unfortunately, it was a situation similar to that in my own English department, where I taught creative writing; often it seemed that lately the very noun "art" had been labeled all but an obscenity on campus, something never to be uttered in those halls lest one be met with accusations of elitism, meaning a lack of suitably stone-faced political correctness and conformity. But if nothing else, in addition to your students being vocally appreciative of the time and attention you gave them at the University of Texas during your appointment there, you did write well in Austin and produced a new volume on your specialty, the most honored writer in Brazilian literary history, Machado de Assis, a nineteenth-century novelist so stylistically prescient for his day (*Epitaph of a Small Winner*, *Quincas Borba*, and others) that when the dazzling era of late-twentieth-century experimental writing in the U.S. boomed, innovators such as John Barth, Donald Barthelme, and Susan Sontag practically lined up to take turns in paying tribute to Machado's vision and achievement: in Machado there appeared to be a valid Joyce or Faulkner well before there was any Joyce or Faulkner. Which made it all the more absurd, how with this chairperson's own research entailing something as inherently topical as it was, she had suggested, quite unbelievably, that your own research wasn't matching the current interests of the department in its study of Spanish and Portuguese writing. Then, upon your return to São Paulo, the new book on Machado de Assis you wrote and published while in Austin received the highest honor your country can give to a work of literary criticism, the top prize from the Brazilian Academy of Letters, an equivalent of our Pulitzer or National Book Award and including a generous cash honorarium; so your research on Brazilian literature, if not important in a seemingly misinformed academic department in the faraway U.S., was completely in line with what was deemed important in *Brazil*. However, as said, we don't talk about that much anymore, all of it happening two years prior, unless I bring it up. And to see you now with your family and happily productive with your bright and entirely engaging colleagues at the university here in the vibrant, thriving world city of São Paulo, I myself wonder how you even managed to survive as long as you did in a place like provincial Austin, Texas. I mean, no matter all the hype Austin has gotten recently touting its hipness—largely from noisy local real estate developers and chamber of commerce citizenry, or twenty-somethings whose chief mission in life apparently is to indulgently party as much as they can and listen to mediocre live bar music, usually having moved there expressly for those purposes about two months before—the city remains second tier and actually rather conservative deep down, especially when compared to any genuinely progressive sizable American city on either of the coasts. Austin *is* in Texas, after all, and there are the plain and simple hard facts to remember: for instance, the whole state's enthusiastic NRA gun culture ("campus carry" is the policy at the University of Texas), also staunch religious fundamentalists on state education boards wackily redacting school-approved textbooks according to proclaimed creationism, etc.

■

The dashboard panel glows green in the darkened car; we pass slowly through shadowy streets of the old Barra Funda district west of downtown, the darkness there interrupted only occasionally by the spill of bright streetlight sifting through the leaf-laden limbs of the neighborhood's many trees. The engine hums alternatingly higher and lower as you work the stubby stick shift. We pass through more shadowy streets.

■

But we're lost, as it turns out, and you have no idea exactly where Rua Lopes Chaves is.

You spot a brightly lit Shell gas station ahead of us and pull into the corner place, saying somebody there is sure to know. From the car I watch as you go into the station's convenience store and chat with a teenage girl in a crisp red-and-yellow uniform, complete with matching cap—elaborate company uniforms are the order of the day in Brazilian gas stations, a touch that has virtually disappeared in the U.S. The skinny, smiling girl, her large eyes liquid brown, is responsible for tending to the gas pumps, and though we are not purchasing, she nevertheless walks out with you and at the car repeats what she has just told you, that, alas and maybe remarkably—serendipity, all right—we are at the very corner of Rua Lopes Chaves and that the street we have been driving on is, in fact, *Rua Mário de Andrade*. She points to the street sign on the splintery phone pole and says that while narrow Rua Lopes Chaves is one-way, we can surely just put the car in reverse and back our way along it, rather than circling the few blocks to attempt to get access via what she admits is a somewhat confusing intersection at the other end of empty Rua Lopes Chaves.

And that is just what you do, hesitantly maneuvering in reverse the little black Volks—it has imitation wire-wheel hubcaps, a lot of chrome, its attempt at sportiness exaggerated and the kind of car you yourself would never buy, you have explained, but your older son bought it then decided he didn't like it, so what were you to do but purchase it from him, or bail him out, actually?—and zigzagging some in the process of more hesitant and very jerky backing up, parked cars on either side and both of us pivoting our necks the best we can to see where we are going, you laugh and say that you hope no stern São Paulo cop drives by to witness the slapstick performance. The street is dark, with several old masonry homes and also a warehouse or two, newer, and getting out of the car on opposite sides, we both look up at the same time to recognize from the pictures in books and even online that this is the house indeed. There is a lit, open-front *boteco* bar across the corner here at the far end of Rua Lopes Chaves, where the rough types drinking their tall brown bottles of Skol or Brahma beer at plastic tables in front apparently do notice us, you and me, two men in sport jackets standing on the sidewalk of a narrow side street and gazing in appreciation at a house in the moonlight that is strong enough to cast long shadows, big shredded clouds tumbling across the night sky now and then, too.

Perfect.

■

Mário de Andrade's longtime home in this nondescript neighborhood—today seeming industrial rather than residential—sits on the street's far corner; it is a yellow-stucco, two-story place with louvered blue shutters and a central peaked gable, the roof of deep red tile. A white iron fence, low and spiked, surrounds the few square yards of the little garden in front; there's a small entry portico, while above the door's arch stretches a painted script for a welcoming invocation, your finger now pointing up to follow what it says:

Oficina da Palavra

Workshop of the Word, and you speak aloud the literal English translation as we continue to gaze at the house. You add that while it appears to be the name of a government cultural program that maintains the house and possibly uses it for literary sessions and public events, the appellation is very suitable to the spirit of de Andrade himself, who did create many lasting words at this site when he moved here with his mother after his father died. De Andrade was of mixed-race lineage, a "mulatto" (the term was regularly used in multicultural Brazil, once not offensive), and grew up in a well-to-do family; most likely gay, a tall, bespectacled man with a high forehead and the strong features of a stage actor, he was probably referred to in his day as a confirmed bachelor, the way that somebody who couldn't comfortably announce his sexuality in those intolerant other times simply would let people place him in that more

THE WORLD IS A BOOK, INDEED

socially acceptable category of confirmed bachelor. He studied at the São Paulo Conservatory of Drama and Music then taught music composition there, balanced his constant writing of poetry, fiction, and journalism with the job. His avant-garde novel *Macunaíma* (1928) became the work he remains best known for, even if the book—drawing on his ethnographic studies of the Brazilian jungle interior and its native ways as applied to modernism, innovative on that front alone—for me maybe doesn't measure up to the tour de force that is the earlier *Paulicéia desvairada*, eventually given full recognition after his death as an inarguably major document of twentieth-century world literature and one produced—as already mentioned, and so impressively—when only in his twenties.

You explain to me that you think he lived here continuously most of his adult years, except for a brief period in Rio de Janeiro when he took a position at the federal university there following his troubled work as director of the São Paulo Department of Culture; the directorship was a risky role that entailed playing a never-ending political cat-and-mouse game to champion and promote valid art and also manage to keep the job without being outright fired during an era dominated by the right-wing military dictator Getúlio Vargas. You tell me it was probably here at home where he suffered the heart attack in 1945 that killed him at the age of—you calculate the dates in your head, when he was born and when he died—fifty-two or fifty-three, not old at all. We walk around the place, and we admire the elegant nineteenth-century architecture: there are decorative embossed panels set into the facade's masonry, a deeper tan color against the prevailing yellow, also the fine carved-stone balustrade of the central balcony overlooking the street. I suppose we talk not only of de Andrade but other things as well.

I talk about our friend Thiago Nicodemo, mentioning him because a de Andrade connection comes to mind. With the good looks of maybe a Latin American playboy and certainly not seeming the usual awkwardly introverted academic, tall Thiago is polite, outgoing, and amazingly well read, a young scholar of Brazilian cultural history, author of two books on the subject; I first met him when he came to visit you in Austin and give a talk while you were teaching there. I have spent considerable time with him here in São Paulo, and I now tell you about Thiago's lovely girlfriend Bianca, honey-haired and gray-eyed, an art historian employed by a government arts agency, and how she explained in her whispery voice to me—when I met with her and Thiago earlier that week for a day of museum-going and in the course of that I announced my own obsession with de Andrade's work—yes, Bianca explained that she had recently written the copy for an illustrated catalog of the books in this very house, de Andrade's own personal library. You say you must meet her, would definitely like to know more about that, see the catalog for yourself, of course.

We separate and walk around some more, individually studying the house in the moonlight, very pleased with it all; just being where a man of de Andrade's enormous talent lived and worked provides, in a spooky way, a proximity to his creative genius, I tell myself, what often can happen whenever one visits the home or even the grave of a famous writer. Which is when I return from where I have been looking around the back of the place, a stark high-rise abutting the property there, and you say to me, smiling, "Look, there's our friend." It's the girl in the neat red-and-yellow uniform with the puffy cap who gave us directions at the Shell station.

∎

And then did I actually see what happened happen? Could anything be more perfect in describing you, what I knew made you quite unlike anybody I had ever known, to be honest, the sheer kindness you could exude, a quality again illustrated in that simple exchange with a skinny, big-eyed teenage girl who worked at a São Paulo Shell station?

∎

In the shadows, she is leaning back against a high stone wall around the corner from the station here on Rua Chaves Lopes, one knee cocked and the sneaker sole against the wall, a cigarette in her hand. She puffs, looks at us and smiles, and poutingly puffs again.

You go over to her and thank her again for giving us careful instructions for backing up here on the one-way street, and she smiles wider, probably having observed for herself your awkward performance when driving the Volks in such comically zigzagging reverse. You ask her name, and she tells you Teresa. You say to her, Teresa, that it is a very nice name, which she seems to like to hear; you also ask if she's helped others looking for the house the way she helped us, and she says yes, she has helped many of them, people often come looking for the home of this man whoever he is, which she really isn't sure of. And she seems to appreciate your asking her that, too, even taking the time to talk to her. It is the same gentle, smiling, and very kind manner I have observed in your dealing with students, also in your dealing with everybody from custodians and secretaries to bigwig administrators out at the university's new suburban campus, all the sleek, tropically modern classroom buildings there on winding lanes lined with columns of shading palm trees. Why, it is the same way you dealt with those poor women who, in matching T-shirts and baseball caps (more uniforms), endlessly march up and down through the stopped traffic at lights in São Paulo, trying to hand out advertising flyers; when one of them approached us, on the short drive to your home after you picked me up at the subway station earlier, you rolled down the window, took two of the sheets from her, cheerily told her how pretty she was even if she wasn't at all pretty, then explained to me that they got paid by the number of flyers they passed out and you always wanted to help them. You now ask the girl from the gas station if she likes her job, and she flicks the ash of the cigarette in her hand held low, one knee still cocked and sneaker sole still flat on the wall she's leaning against, that little cap set at a jaunty angle atop her bobbed hair; she says it's OK, but she explains that whenever she wants to take a break for a smoke—she puts on a cute frown, a wrinkling of the brow under the cap's short red bill—her boss makes her go around the corner this way to do it—she shakes her head—because he doesn't like her smoking near the gas pumps. And after she leaves, returning to the station, you translate her talk for me, what I missed in the chatty Portuguese, and we both laugh, agreeing wholeheartedly with the boss that it *most definitely* is not the best idea to be smoking around gas pumps.

In front of the yellow house again, standing on the cracked sidewalk, we talk more about de Andrade, talk about other writers, too. We maybe talk again about Hemingway and about Faulkner and about Fitzgerald, the subjects of my upcoming lectures; we even find ourselves talking about Stephen King, your bringing him up more than once lately and, absolutely open-minded as always, thinking more about him as a writer. You argue for his value on the strength of his intensely detailed descriptive passages alone, at times powerfully impressionistic in portraying something like a run-down little factory town in impoverished Maine, plus the dizzying, near Balzacian amount of his production, somebody to be admired on that count alone, though you admit that you personally don't buy into the hokey horror-movie premises of many of his novels; you say that you must track down more writing by him, decide what does hold up in his work. Then we talk again about de Andrade, the kind of undeniable literary bravery he represented in that exciting age of the first full flowering of modernism, as we wonder if such bravery would have any chance of being acknowledged today when too much of supposed literature is simply commercial fare—in truth, King included, which you concede—and if there could even be an event such as Modern Art Week to loudly rattle the whole culture of a nation that way nowadays, de Andrade indisputably brave.

But we agree we have to believe in that, *bravery*, how it is all there really is when everything else is said and done concerning serious literature.

■

I wonder again what the men in western jeans, sport shirts, and leather jackets in the *boteco* across the street on the opposite corner, the rather ramshackle open-front bar, are thinking while they sit there and look at us now maybe getting carried away with our conversation under the

THE WORLD IS A BOOK, INDEED

slow-somersaulting clouds in a sky of rich inky blue, those rough men of the sort who do frequent street-side *botecos?* Do they see us as fools? Do they continue to ask themselves what two grown men are, in fact, doing while standing around on this empty nondescript corner late on a Saturday night and talking very animatedly about who knows what, the two of us smiling, excited, even laughing out loud, echoingly, as I turn the collar of my tweed sport jacket up a bit, because as lovely as the night is, it is getting cooler? Do they hear you say (and your voice, always relaxed and melodically sibilant, does come back to me now, there is no losing it in the softening folds of memory or the camouflage of summary narration while I write this in my apartment in Austin a year later, only direct dialogue can capture it) what you do say, very seriously?

"Peter, what would we have if we didn't have literature?"

■

Hell, it is all wonderful, this night.

■

And with that, we return to the little box of a black VW, its garish overdosing of chrome trim and the hopefully sporty, but pretty goofy, imitation wire-wheel hubcaps. You tell me we must see more of the city, you tell me we will *eventually* get back to the Hotel Itamarati, not to worry, as we do set out to explore so much of the city and begin driving and driving like that.

■

We pass through a very tony urban neighborhood—darkened streets again and large residences behind high protecting walls topped with shards of jagged glass—and move along slowly in the car. We come upon the major soccer stadium in the city proper, the handsome Estádio do Pacaembu, home of the Sport Club Corinthians Paulista of the revered white-and-black team colors seen on T-shirts everywhere around the city; they're always a national championship contender here in football-mad Brazil. The stadium rises in the center of a velvety asphalt parking lot, the venue surely futuristic for its day when built and looking like something out of a *Flash Gordon* episode; or—this is it—it's the Roman Colosseum as reinterpreted according to the ethos of 1930s fascist utopianism, maybe, with repeated classical arches but streamlined, too, the landscaping all fruit trees and slim emerald cypresses: everything is immaculately groomed, *extremely* upscale, especially for a sports stadium. In the huge parking lot that surrounds it we encounter a gathering of skateboarding teenage kids, dozens of them and both guys and girls. Some grind this way and that on the boards, some sit on the pavement and watch and talk; it's a regular Saturday night meeting spot, an event for them, you suspect, complete with a boom box playing music. The kids on the boards wave at us arcingly, even half somnambulistically, sort of floating along, their being the happy, wheel-rattling angels that they somehow are, as we weave aimlessly around the expanse of the otherwise night-empty lot.

There's another stint on the freeway, brief, and we are next on Avenida Paulista itself, the wide eight lanes of this grand boulevard in a true cavern of lofty skyscrapers. It's the center of business and fashion for the city and probably all of South America today. Economically strong, Brazil in 2012 is very prosperous—despite its pockets of intense poverty, the many favela slums—and the country is actually making loans to assist the faltering EU, I know; even this late the Avenida Paulista is busy, alive. You point out to me a helicopter teeteringly settling down from the sky to alight atop a skyscraper of gleaming steel and tinted glass, because I have mentioned to you before how taken I am with just the idea of all the helicopters of São Paulo, forever shuttling the high-rolling execs back and forth to their offices; and on a Saturday night one such helicopter does appear to be coming into the city to allow somebody to finish up a little extra work in a spacious office high up in that skyscraper and perhaps move more of those millions of dollars around, worldwide. We slowly cruise along with the traffic, from one end of the long concourse, indisputably the Champs-Élysées or Fifth Avenue of the continent, to the other. You look for one of the few old landmark mansions that have survived in this explosion of modernity, the Casa das Rosas, and then sight it on the boulevard, sandwiched to the point of virtually being camouflaged by two high-rises and on a small park-like plot of, appropriately enough, many blossoming rose bushes; the frilled house seems almost a fantasy of a structure, an attractive jumble of gables and porches and a geometrically complicated French mansard slate roof. Several blocks farther on, you point out what you are quite sure is yet another of the handful of remaining mansions of the type that once lined the avenue and were the lavish homes of the wealthy nineteenth-century coffee barons who made São Paulo enormously rich in their own day; this particular mansion is equally frilly and opulent but now—wouldn't you know it—housing a thriving, brightly lit urban McDonald's. Again we get on the looping freeway of more whizzing cars and streakily bleeding red taillights, and then we are back in the very heart of Centro, off the freeway for good and entering the district of the cathedral and the university's Faculty of Law; important in Brazilian history, academically eminent, the Faculty of Law offers a quiet square where everything is beyond deserted, a scene that in its near timelessness—the classical pillars of the buff stone law school building, the black-and-white-tiled pavement, the watchful figures of sculpted statues atop solid pedestals—is straight out of a de Chirico painting. You explain to me in more detail, when I ask, what you have told me earlier, how you began your own study there, training to become a lawyer as a precocious eighteen-year-old scholarship boy and son of a country doctor in the interior state of Minas Gerais, before realizing that, of course, literature was what you *had* to study, would be what you wanted to spend your *life* with, so you abandoned law and worked on degrees at the Faculty of Letters across town.

But after so much driving, seeing so much, we both concede it is getting late, very late, and we should work our way through the maze of old streets in Centro, back to the Hotel Itamarati on the little boulevard of Avenida Vieira de Carvalho. Calmly commercial during the day with its restaurants and many shops, Avenida Vieira de Carvalho is later, after nightfall, the epicenter of São Paulo's gay and wildly transvestite scene, not only on a Saturday but every night beginning to fill at ten or so, noisy, something I have learned all too well in my couple of weeks at the hotel. Luckily, I tell you, my room is upper floor and in the back, can seem miles away from what's below, the usual loud street commotion.

You are the one who now asks me, almost naively, if I think it will be wild tonight, and you admit it has been a while since you spent much time in Centro at night. I tell you it is Saturday, after all, so it should be more than wild tonight, no?

■

(But all this is hopeless. And I am not driving in São Paulo at night with you. I am not because you have died, less than a year after my fine time there in May 2012. And the little explosions that are part of coming to terms with the death of anybody close continue to detonate at unexpected moments, the timbre of your gentle voice remembered, even the whole sadness of what happened reconstructed. And in January, a week after you sent to me in Austin a cheery New Year's email greeting, with best wishes from you and Marlene, there soon followed the somber news from others and the rather frantic exchange of emails among those of us who knew you, all of us stunned, nobody knowing what to say about the fact that apparently you had unexpectedly fainted at home and had been taken to the hospital for routine tests. The diagnosis was very serious, an advanced stage of cancer. After that everything became that much more accelerated. First the optimistic reports that there had been radical surgery, removal of parts of your stomach, intestine, and pancreas, yet the operation turned out well, we were told; Marlene and your adult sons, Ivan and João, they all confirmed you were uncomplaining during the painful ordeal, the prognosis for recovery from a disease like pancreatic cancer that is seldom good was, in this case, thankfully and quite miraculously good indeed—and then three days after that, on January 31, the email notification from Thiago Nicodemo, the young scholar, simply giving me the hollow message there on my laptop screen that "Our friend has passed away," some explanation from Thiago of a liver infection picked up in the hospital in the course of recovery from the surgery, but no explanation making any sense whatsoever, grief-stricken Thiago admitted. The next few days various Brazilian online news sites ran obituaries. I read them over and over, going from one to another; there was much talk about your having been one of the most respected scholars and teachers in the entire nation, also mention of your time at the University of Texas. Which did anger me some, to think again how shabbily you were treated there and how that treatment made for a telling comment on the overall lamentable state of the study of literature in American universities today, caught up in examining writing as if a matter of sociology or political science, too often bordering on outright polemic for a commentary propagating a set personal agenda; and while such concerns can certainly have obvious value and significance, they had displaced a well-rounded approach and moved, as said, toward exclusivity, the *only* things important in literature, as accompanied by the stifling, self-righteous authoritarian undercurrent any critical myopia breeds. In that atmosphere, supposed serious literary analysis on the topic of dildos might be considered to have more worth than what has always been the unique, mysterious, and humanely moving power of words themselves and *art*. Even the students seemed to realize that once the magic is taken out of literature it loses much of its essential appeal, possibly a prime reason why the number of undergraduate majors in many English departments was dramatically dwindling in comparison to that of other liberal arts disciplines, sometimes heading toward about half of what it had once been. Knowing that the custom of Brazil is for swift funeral services and burial, I was not ready to read in one online obituary that there had been a cremation the very next day, which just reinforced and loudly echoed the impact of the stark truth that you were absolutely gone, were suddenly *nothing*. I think if it were even a situation of your corporeal remains existing in the darkness of a good mahogany coffin lined with soft, pleated white satin, let's say, that would be *something*, everything wouldn't be so unfair and inalterable and ultimately *unreal.* I had strange dreams about you, seeing the two of us in São Paulo; I remembered how we visited in what could have been only a dream itself the Workshop of the Word that night, the scripted greeting above the door of Mário de Andrade's residence announcing exactly that. And I started to think more of what you said then, the line spoken by you declaratively while we stood on the sidewalk becoming the single one that still seems to remain for me in the formal framing of quotation marks as I write this now, "Peter, what would we have if we didn't have literature?" For some reason—besides the dreaming, and this perhaps not so odd—I went farther back in time, my thoughts triggered by those words you had spoken that night. I pictured myself when young and in college, in the bedroom of the suite of rooms in Quincy House, my dorm at Harvard. And at the desk there, adjusting the flex-arm lamp, I was reading the heavy, blue-bound *Norton Anthology of English Literature,* specifically the rhapsody of Shelley's "Adonais." It's the poem that addresses directly the loss of his friend Keats, and in the tradition of many revered poems in literary history, it sets out, nobly and with building conviction, to ward off the looming presence of death following the loss of a friend very dear. I read the long poem repeatedly back then, a favorite of mine. I was young and I was completely convinced that, no question about it, words and literature could do anything. And there was the way the disheveled professor in his rumpled suit in the small seminar classroom in Harvard's Sever Hall, the old silver steam-heat radiators coughing, chalked an extended horizontal stroke on the dusty blackboard, a long line to represent chronological time; next, perpendicular to that and in a vertical stroke equally as long, he chalked another line to represent the infinite transcendence of any single moment, telling the dozen of us, all male, wearing suit jackets and ties and seated there facing him, that if one enters onto that vertical line with the power of art—as Keats, who in the poem is called "Adonais," surely did in his own work, Shelley says, with the name Adonais itself a variation on Adonis, youthfully handsome and killed by the boar in classical mythology—one will possibly escape the doleful, cruelly incessant whisperings of clocks and fading days. Shelley struggles *very* hard but gradually does come to terms with Keats's early death in Italy, and he finally asserts that with the writing of his brilliant poems, Keats is maybe still out there somewhere on the vertical line, a place where the horizontal line holds no sway over him—"What Adonais is, why fear we to become?" True, "Adonais" is one in a long list of well-known works by poets challenging death while armed with the power of art alone, notable among them Abraham Cowley, whose verse "Dark as the grave wherein my friend is laid" became the title of the lyrically poignant Malcolm Lowry novel, as well as Tennyson in his moving, often quoted "In Memoriam" and, most masterly, Milton in the poem scholars regard as the greatest of all pastoral elegies in English literature, "Lycidas." But after you died in that hospital in São Paulo, with me no longer a hopeful twenty-year-old student in Quincy House and now older—very much so, *older*—I suddenly found myself not believing any of it, I found myself questioning the whole egotistical and perhaps inconsequential quest of literature itself that I had probably wasted too much of my own life on, letting it eat up the years while I neglected too many other things at its expense, something that haunted me more and more in recent years. Which meant, in turn, that I found myself just repeatedly picturing so clearly that cozily warm cubbyhole bedroom high up under the eaves in redbrick Quincy House in the Massachusetts winter—the cracked, maize-colored walls, the slab of an old oaken dorm desk, the cone of light from the flex-arm lamp illuminating the fine print of the tissuey pages of the big *Norton Anthology*—and seeing myself, I admitted, as but a college kid then yet already a confirmed fool, not only in my youthful vanity, believing myself prepared to figure out things in my own life in terms of the greats like Shelley and Keats, but also in refusing to concede the obvious when it came to literature, what now hit me rock-hard—the heavy and ultimately futile *meaninglessness* of it all.)

■

(But what if right here, writing at this moment, I can say differently? What if I can change everything by just tapping away at the black keyboard of this MacBook Pro and let the white electronic page bordered by its royal blue and rising slowly before me tell a different story altogether? What if I write it so that it reads another way, meaning I will write it now so that the illness will never happen to you, that there will never be what there is and, so, maybe there *isn't?* Which is to say, reality is what could be but an odd dream of you and Marlene first being given the results of the tests by the doctors, their explaining that the future for anybody diagnosed with pancreatic cancer is seldom hopeful, then the supposedly successful operation, before the total and most unexpected reversal and death several days later from something as random as a minor hospital infection, your name soon appearing in online obituaries. The obituaries talked at length of you as an authority on Machado de Assis, an acknowledged giant in nineteenth-century South American literature. One pointed out your annotated edition, which had become a popular classroom text, of the most important writer of the Portuguese language, Camões, author of the epic *The Lusiads,* a tale in which the supremely visionary sailor/poet probed a subject no less than the large mystery of the oceans themselves during that heady sixteenth century of his, the great age of Portuguese exploration and the fleets of wave-braving, sail-billowing caravels venturing in his compellingly resonant verse to the quite unknown ends of the earth—and, in your thinking, I liked to believe, to possibly the far extremities and utmost reaches of the human soul as well. Still, what if those obituaries, too, are something I *never* read, and everything—the doctors and the hospital and the praising obituaries—is only that, in the category of the merely dreamt, if I do simply now *write* life happening another way, give it substance according to that and denying with all my strength the insubstantiality of the sadly limited number of years any one of us inevitably is allotted, just so much precious oxygen to be breathed, before all is eventually gone maybe before it even began? So as I sit before the keyboard I do compose this to say it happened another way. I reproduce—or have reproduced—the scenes of our night in São Paulo in this essay, but, in my creating such a night with strings of words and the accumulating sentences, I now decide that I can also choose to give it permanence and not have it end, I will indeed have us keep on driving some more in São Paulo at night, never stopping in the speeding Volks and therefore never surrendering to what might, or what will, happen. We *are* on the freeway, and we *are* perpetually looping the vast city with its forest of skyscrapers, São Paulo under the moon of the Southern Cone so full and glowingly buttery above that I can't help but suspect again that none of anything is real and somebody could be putting me on—no moon is *that big*, no distant skyline is *that lit and dazzling* in the rich, rich dark blue of the autumn night? And, oh, how we do keep driving and driving!)

■

Though of course we *don't* keep driving, that is not the way it is.

■

Because the way it is, is that we are now proceeding at a crawling pace in the black Volkswagen Golf through the empty narrow streets of the old downtown, buildings baroque upon baroque. We pass the Theatro Municipal, an ornate and imposingly massive opera house that actually was the site of the Modern Art Week in 1922, where Mário de Andrade took his stand with his young and intrepid cohorts; we even pass the art deco main municipal library nearby, a sturdy gray granite block of a building on meticulously landscaped grounds, which today bears the name of none other than de Andrade himself; we cross Avenida Ipiranga and pass the park there, Praça da República, with its rustic footbridges and silhouettes of spindly, mop-headed palm trees, to find ourselves at last and this late, past midnight, on Avenida Vieira de Carvalho.

And you certainly are struck by the carnival atmosphere, the gay scene on a Saturday night. The *botecos* that one hardly notices in daytime are now packed and noisy, and at a couple of street corners vendors have set up sidewalk pushcarts to serve neon-colored mixed drinks, techno-rock music blaring from the open doors of a club somewhere; it is a large crowd of gay men and the many transvestites, too. The latter have blond wigs and redhead wigs; they're artistically made up with the kind of care to put any runway fashion model to shame, plenty of wobbly high heels and skintight dresses, even lamé. We sit in the dark of the car, parked across the street from the Hotel Itamarati, and the green dashboard lights continue to glow lowly on our faces, nothing but masks in that darkness; we agree that the driving has been great, and you look around between the bucket seats, tell me to make sure I have everything—my sunglasses and my Bic pen and especially the little pocket notebook with a blue marbleized cover where, in fact, I had been taking a few pages of notes there at the Casa de Mário de Andrade, jotting down details of the place. We talk about how you will call me the next day, Sunday, to give me the exact time in the morning that the government SUV from the university will come to the Hotel Itamarati to pick me up and take me to the suburban campus for my first lecture on Monday, your saying that you have heard word that a full seventy-five people have signed up to attend the talks and there will be a surprisingly large turnout. I joke that at least I won't be like the last guy they brought in to participate in this yearlong series of international visiting lecturers to celebrate the fiftieth anniversary of the university's press; he was a Frenchman, you've told me, who spoke on bibliography and drew an audience of only seven or eight confused souls.

Speaking to you from the sidewalk before I leave, through the open window while I lean over in my khakis and old tweed sport jacket, smiling, I say again I feel good knowing I won't do as badly as the unfortunate Frenchman, that's for sure.

■

Past the loud crowd, then entering the airy open lobby of the Hotel Itamarati—oversize black leather easy chairs and low tables piled with the day's newspapers—I see that the guys in proper blazers who are the hotel staff at the reception desk are now themselves relaxing this late on a Saturday night, ties tugged loose at the collar; a heavily lipsticked blond transvestite with a paste-on beauty mark is casually chatting with them, a remarkably passable Marilyn Monroe look-alike. They all nod to me, friendly. I take the chugging little elevator to my room high up on the seventh floor in back, number 704, where it is quiet, the street and its noise left far behind.

I switch on the lamp next to the bed. I push open the old French window wide to the big Brazilian night. In the pink-tiled bathroom I splash some water on my face, dry it with a fresh towel lifted from the stack. The mini-refrigerator ceases its low grumbling in a truncated clunk and suddenly the room is absolutely silent. (*There are two mirrors in the room, and I suppose they are watching all of this, tossing reflections of me back and forth to each other, lightly, fragilely.*) I go to the little dresser-desk where there is a stack of maps, books, and bulging manila envelopes with notes for my lectures and photocopied handouts, and I look for the volume of de Andrade's verse, *Paulicéia desvairada,* its title most aptly translated as *Hallucinated City.* A clothbound dual-language edition, the book is from the university library in Austin, a faded moss-green hardcover and published by Vanderbilt University Press in 1968, the dirty white label on its spine giving the long Dewey decimal number. I gently lob it to the flower-print bedspread, thinking I might do some rereading of the poems in bed after I undress to T-shirt and boxer shorts and turn down the spread and sheets, savor some of those lines yet again. But already I am feeling suddenly and pleasantly exhausted, and I decide that I am really too tired, don't have the energy and won't read before I finally doze off.

Yes, before I do fall asleep and enter into what is for me the good dream of you, Ivan Prado Teixeira, and the two of us driving maybe forever through the sweet and very faraway city of São Paulo at night.

—*Southern Review,* 2016

Honorary Africanist

SIMPLY PUT, it was 1979 and I was young.

And maybe most important for me at the time, I was wild about African literature.

For over a year I had been immersing myself in books from the continent, much of it as contained in the fine British paperbacks of those iconic orange-and-white covers and paper like newsprint of the Heinemann African Literature Series. The series's editorial advisor was no less a novelist than the eminent Nigerian Chinua Achebe, and it offered just about all the seminal modern African writing then, with acknowledged masters such as James Ngugi from Kenya and Ousmane Sembène from Senegal and a long list of South Africans, including Alex La Guma, Bessie Head, and Peter Abrahams.

There was a daring to African literature, both in its language and forms entirely fresh, plus the deep political commitment of writers willing to face directly very big issues, pro and con, in the continent's heady emergence into the world scene after independence. It could make too much recent writing from America and Europe sometimes look routine in its safe domesticity. Or, as a friend of mine used to say about any writing that seemed only more of the same, novels often touted by the media and noisy advertising machine—in the U.S., anyway—as ultimately major and having "must read" status, yet upon that reading turning out to be the usual safe, by-the-numbers fare: "Just time at the beach."

African literature, and definitely my own discovery of it, was flat-out exciting.

∎

Soon I was longing to travel to Africa myself to learn firsthand more about that literature, and I suppose I worked sort of a bluff, though hopefully ethical enough. I was teaching creative writing at Iowa State, my first regular university appointment (as opposed to come-and-go visiting stints) after the bust of a brief career as a daily-newspaper reporter.

There was a generous older couple who were the African-lit scholars on campus, one in the English department, one in the French. They told me that despite my having snuck into academia by the back door as a so-called creative writer, absolutely sans PhD, not even an MFA and no qualifying experience whatsoever as an academic researcher, I just might be able to receive a summer research grant from the university to fund my interest—or probably better termed my *fixation* by that point. In the course of my extensive reading, I had written a short piece on a powerfully autobiographical novel I'd come across, Dugmore Boetie's *Familiarity Is the Kingdom of the Lost* (1969). Subtitled "The Story of a Black Man in South Africa," the book recounts the strange life of an orphan later turned criminal surviving in the outer margins of a society that due to the harrowing injustice of apartheid has been rendered beyond Kafkaesque, bordering on fully hallucinatory. If for no other reason than to see if I could do some good and generate more readers for a little-known novel, I submitted on spec the short reconsideration of it to *Africa Today*; it was a journal I'd been poring through, issue after old issue, in the stacks of the Iowa State library. Surprisingly, they accepted it.

That single publication proved my ticket. I somehow landed the grant on the basis of only the eight hundred or so published words on Boetie as a sample of my (I realize this sounds far-fetched) "research" in the field of African literature along with what I can say was a very spirited several-page proposal to investigate the literature of Cameroon specifically, interviewing writers there. The couple who were my mentors, the Africanists (as those in the field are called), had recommended that Cameroon would be a perfect place to go for somebody on a first trip to Africa, one-stop shopping, if you will, with plenty of variety. The independent country had been formed by the merger of a former French colony and a former British one, and geographically it sat in an ideal spot, nestled at the crook of Africa itself; the northern tip of its triangular shape touched the Sahara's edge by Chad, a territory of camel-herding Muslim nomads, and the long southern base was solidly in the central jungle of the continent, where animist Pygmy tribes inhabited the scattered thatched villages. Best of all, owing to lively intellectual activity in the two main cities where I'd be—Doula on the Atlantic coast and the inland central capital, Yaoundé—the country had emerged as somewhat of a literary powerhouse in sub-Saharan Africa, its writers winning important awards abroad.

So, that June I boarded an Air France 707 in Marseilles. I sat in the plane for the hours of the engines droning on and on over the undulatingly patterned red-orange sands of a Sahara Desert that could look like an odd, half-dreamt sea indeed from up there in the almost too-clear blue, heading to the Republic of Cameroon.

On the near empty flight I was joined in my row of seats by a rather comic roly-poly Britisher in a rumpled gray suit. A salesman for industrial plastic pipe and right out of a Graham Greene novel, he regaled me with tales of his various illnesses incurred while selling in Africa, warning me I should be *extremely* careful. He said that once while in Lagos he had stocked a supply of bottles of purified water in his hotel room's mini-refrigerator, and he would swear to this day that the guy cleaning his room merrily helped himself to one and then refilled the bottle with tap water straight from the sink faucet.

"I drank it and was flat on my arse the next day, then a week later I had to be shipped back to the Hospital for Tropical Diseases in London, I did."

A late takeoff had delayed the arrival time by several hours, and I missed my continuing flight from Doula to Yaoundé, so Air France put me up in an upscale hotel for the night. I went to the downstairs bar for a beer and had a hard time getting my room key back from a cute and cheery petite girl in a green cocktail dress working the territory as a hooker. She slid onto the barstool next to me and snatched the key with its large tag from my trousers' pocket (I guess the m.o. was to lead you up to your room while dangling it), some joking conversation ensuing and my explaining to her in French I really wasn't interested in such recreation, until she eventually did return it.

Both encounters—the admonishing Britisher, the friendly hooker—

were a good indication that I didn't have much experience in this kind of unpredictable travel (I'd gone on annual spring tours with my college rugby team to play matches in the former Commonwealth Caribbean, and I'd bounced around Europe and lived for a year in Ireland writing fiction and doing freelance newspaper work, that was about it), though nevertheless, what I did know was that I was more than excited to be there, in Africa at long last.

Early the next morning I flew on to Yaoundé.

■

Yaoundé proved to be a lovely city up in the central mountains. The French had originally located their capital there rather than in the major shipping port of steamy Doula because of the clear air and milder climate. The *centre-ville* consisted of old colonial administration buildings with shading porticoes, also a few modernistic stubby high-rises built by the French and the decidedly avant-garde Catholic cathedral, a city landmark; dented yellow taxis beep-beeped away, and the surrounding clustered neighborhoods of tin-roofed houses spread out in every direction on lumpy green mountains spider-webbed with red-dirt roads. The air itself smelled half of open sewage and half of the flowering trees, the two together somehow completely right, an authentic tropical fragrance, I decided. I booked into a small two-story hotel on a steep road and directly across from a white-stuccoed military club identified as the Officers' Mess; a pair of immaculately khaki-uniformed soldiers with Uzis, stone-faced, were always on guard at its front drive. (During my stay, a painting crew materialized one day to energetically give the Officers' Mess a quick coat of fresh whitewash, using fat rollers on long wooden poles; the city was getting spruced up for an official state visit of a VIP from the French government that week, though most of that white just as quickly washed off and into the overflowing gutter during the first heavy downpour two or three days later.) When one of the writers I'd contacted ahead of time, Marcien Towa, a Paris-educated philosopher at the University of Yaoundé, stopped by with a couple of students to welcome me, smiling and friendly, we talked in my low-budget and functional—at best—room in the hotel; he looked around, frowned, and concluded: "This will never do." He asked me to hand him the phone, and after several minutes of relaxed chat with the person on the other end of the line, he hung up and told me it was all arranged: I could move into a much more suitable apartment in a comfortable modern compound maintained for UNESCO staffers. I asked him who he'd been speaking to on the phone.

"Oh, him, he is our minister of education, always a help in matters of this sort."

At a moment like that, maybe even I harbored a shred of belief I was a bona fide scholar, and one deserving of top-of-the-line treatment, no?

Word spread that there was an American in Cameroon investigating the country's literature. It seemed that no sooner would I meet up with one writer for an interview than he would suggest that I simply had to meet another, an introduction ensuing. Some of these writers, as with Towa, I'd read in depth when back in Iowa. I'd typed letters to them on those tissue-thin, complicatedly folded "air letter" contraptions that used to be popular for overseas communication, their flimsiness alone suggesting they most likely would never arrive; fortunately, most of mine did. The tool of my supposed interviewing trade was a bulky, battery-operated Panasonic tape recorder the size of a cigar box I'd stuffed in my single piece of luggage, a brown vinyl carry-on flight bag with a lot of zippered outside pockets and purchased from a Times Square mail order shop for $7.95. Also packed were a few changes of clothes, books by the writers I would meet with, and, very important to me, two matching diary-style notebooks with leatherette covers, a red and a black. The red contained the voluminous notes I had been diligently taking that entire spring on my African reading and titled rather histrionically on the first page, as I remember it, "BIG AFRICA." The black was the journal I would keep while there, mostly about my meetings with writers as well as documentation of my daily wanderings and the random larger thoughts triggered by all that, too. Religiously, I made the lengthy entries each evening while I sat out on the balcony in my apartment at the

UNESCO compound overlooking a patch of veritable jungle, with monkeys and frogs and who knows how many thousands of varieties of bugs offering their collective choral racket and me scribbling away, Bic ballpoint in hand. The title on the first page of that black notebook could have been a little over the top, too, in its haughty if juvenile simplicity: "THE TRIP."

■

Who did I meet with?

I met with the leading playwright in Cameroon, Guillaume Oyono-Mbia. Forty or so and with an actor's confidence about him—handsome, deep-voiced—he wore a crisp blazer and slacks. He'd had success with a string of comically satiric plays that worked well both on stage and over the radio. They were usually about the clash of old tribal traditions with the new realities of Africa, and the titles alone could serve as compact plot summaries, such as *Three Suitors: One Husband* and *Our Daughter Will Not Marry!* We sat at an outdoor cafe enclosed in trellises thick with scarlet bougainvillea, the city traffic growling by. We talked not only about his plays but also what could often be the complicated issue of languages in Cameroon. The country was the sole one in Africa officially bilingual, according to its 1961 founding constitution, and even classes at the university were taught sometimes in English, sometimes in French. Oyono-Mbia was known to write in both, perhaps Beckettian on that count. Of course, there were many tribal languages of the various regions as well, and to complicate the polyglot stew more, Germany, once with ambitious colonial dreams of its own and forays into Africa prior to World War I, had taken over the territory for a while (Kamerun). Probably outdoing the French in choice of affable climate, the Germans built their own capital, Buea, on the slopes of the lofty pyramidal rise of volcanic Mount Cameroon; at nearly 14,000 feet it was the highest mountain on the west side of the continent. (I would later visit Buea on my trip; the town was an oddity with some Bavarian architecture set among tall pines at that altitude, certainly not one's stock image of sub-Saharan Africa and a look more readily associated with lederhosen and bouncy accordion polkas, I'd say.) Oyono-Mbia explained to me that some of the old people, like his grandparents in their rural village, still spoke German but had no word for "airplane" because the invention didn't come into general use until after the Germans fled in 1916. He said that even today they employed a ready equivalent to describe what they saw whenever a silver jet hissed above them in the sky.

"In German they will call it, naturally enough, 'the thing that flies,'" Oyono-Mbia laughed.

I met with the poet Ernest Alima. A polite, good-natured younger man, he worked in a government translation office. He had published just one book of poetry, quite well received, *Si tu veux vivre longtemps* (*If You Want to Live a Long Time*, 1977) and would go on to be recognized as one of the seminal figures in the country's postcolonial literature. With Ernest it wasn't only the initial interview, though there was good talk then of the tradition of African verse and such, its oral origins and the influence of indigenous rhythms, and after the taping session we became pretty good friends during my stay. Ernest was determined that I should see the full panorama of Yaoundé life and voluntarily assumed the role of impromptu guide. One afternoon we planned to meet at the ceremonial opening of a small roadside bookstore in a dusty neighborhood, Mvog-Ada; Ernest had arranged for my invitation. It was a wonderful gathering that spilled outside the store and could have been the equivalent of a literary party anywhere, drinks and snacks set out on tables and plenty of gossip about authors and publishers, all transpiring amid the African rock playing from a rickety open-front bar next door. The national minister of culture was on hand to pontificate after the cutting of the ceremonial ribbon (true, I was traveling in surprisingly high circles, first the minister of education and now the minister of culture) as well as—attracting much more attention—a popular young actress from the national theater. She arrived fashionably late, and the appearance of such a strikingly statuesque beauty in a colorful print robe and matching head wrap was enough to make a noisy male novelist talking with a group of us suddenly pivot almost in mid-sentence and

quickly head her way, to see if he could (his exact words) "chat her up."
Another afternoon, a Saturday, I accompanied Ernest on a walk through
his neighborhood. We repeatedly stopped for him to introduce me to
yet another friend of his, shaking hands, and the rambling included a
visit to a tiny beauty salon in a backstreet run by a woman he'd known
since childhood. There, amid the aroma of heating curlers and pungent
setting chemicals in the cramped, brightly painted place, the few ladies
having their hair done turned to us in unison, an unexpected visit indeed; the proprietress, big comb in hand, stepped forward to smilingly
greet Ernest and then take a long look at me—the old once-over, from
Red Sox baseball cap to scuffed desert boots—as surely an American
had never ventured into her shop before. She melodically pronounced
in French:

"Oh là là, now what do we have here?"

That evening we had dinner at Ernest's home. It was a tin-roof place
in the city with a maze of rooms he shared as a bachelor with relatives.
For each of us there were a couple of ears of corn, fresh-roasted *caca-
huètes* (peanuts), and a tall brown bottle of locally brewed "33" Export
beer served by a gracious young female (maybe a cousin) as we sat on
low, foot-high stools, a simple, healthy, and very fine meal. We later
headed to the far outskirts of the city in a backfiring yellow Toyota taxi,
on our way to a ramshackle large dance hall delightfully named Disco
Satellite 2001. There, more of that African rock—meandering, boun-
cily pinging—played from massive upright floor speakers, the music
resonating deep in your rib cage. At one point everybody cleared the
way for a good-looking teenage boy who was obviously the heartthrob
of the legions of girls on hand. He wore a tight silklike shirt, flashy, and
bell-bottom trousers, classic 1970s platform shoes, too; his hairdo was
an exact replica of the mile-high James Brown "conk," complete with
forehead finger wave. Out on the empty floor he began to dance alone to
the slower music the DJ had put on, rhythmically gyrating and so lithely
cool that he could have been dry ice, while a half-dozen of the prettiest
girls, one by one, moved onto the floor to dance around him. It was as
if each were seductively playing up to him but the boy not paying an

iota of attention to any of them as he continued his own slow, almost hypnotic dancing, simply assuming, it seemed, their adoration existed only to confirm his undeniable and ultimate cool. The performance was apparently a set routine they were all very used to going through every week.

"This guy is great," I said to Ernest, making my voice loud enough to be heard above the music.

"A true Romeo," he said. "And when he is done we will then have you go out there and do the same, a dance, and the girls will all love you, too."

"I doubt that would work."

"I know, I do, too," Ernest said, laughing.

With Ernest there was always a lot of fun.

And, most significant, I met with René Philombe, pseudonym of Philippe-Louis Ombédé; I greatly admired his work. Philombe was probably the best-known writer living in the country at the time. Others had settled in France for political or career reasons, like prominent novelists Mongo Beti and Francis Bebey, while the diplomat/writer Ferdinand Oyono, author of the acclaimed novel *Houseboy* (and no relation to the playwright Oyono-Mbia, it seems), was posted elsewhere on government assignment. In fact, Philombe's life story was close to legendary. A political activist since his teens in the 1940s under French colonial rule, Philombe drifted into an unlikely career, that of a policeman in Doula. It wasn't long, however, before his strong Marxist beliefs resurfaced in his organizing the Cameroonian police for their first national union. Around that time, a spinal disease left his legs paralyzed, and he lost his job with the police force and began writing. He moved to Yaoundé, the scruffy end of the Nlongkak district not far from the *centre-ville*, where he lived in a single room he called his cambuse (hut).

His first book built on the observations of a humble, very kind crippled man who lives alone and meditates on the ways of the world in a series of tales about the neighborhood people he interacts with, *Letters from My Hut* (in French, *Lettres de ma cambuse*). In 1965 the book won a highly regarded international writing award from the Académie

Française, the Prix Mottart, which firmly established Philombe's name as a writer in Cameroon; it was translated into English in 1977. His physical limitations didn't rule out his challenging the corruption of Cameroon's apparently self-assumed president for life, Ahmadou Ahidjo, and he continued to bravely criticize in short-lived opposition newspapers in Yaoundé. To some a "benevolent dictator," President Ahidjo preached inclusivity between the Francophone and smaller Anglophone sectors of the country, and he did manage to present a less harsh image than many African heads of state. Avoiding the standard spangled military uniforms favored by dictators, Ahidjo usually dressed in traditional attire, the long white *boubou* gown and red cap of the country's Muslim north, his home region, and he always added the title El Hajj to his name, indicating he'd made the pilgrimage to Mecca and perhaps his believing such might help project a reverent image. Still, benevolent to some or not, he kept an iron grip on the populace with a secret network of internal spies and tolerated little dissent or questioning of his rule. (Cameroon had no television when I was there, among the last countries in the world not to. Ahidjo reportedly feared that TV might further complicate his efforts to tightly control the news, which he did manage to do with the government-run radio station and national newspaper, both propagandistic and heavily censored. One result of the control, I noticed right off, was how any photo of Ahidjo in public with a group in the newspaper could get doctored via the old-fashioned, literal "cut-and-paste" method to render him, a rather short man, taller than everybody else. But sometimes, possibly in the haste of the paper's deadline, it seemed that the paste job got slapped down too quickly, his raised figure at an angle, so to my eye the man in that flowing white gown and cap would appear dangerously, and comically, akin to the Flying Nun of the old TV series of that name, about to take off.) Continuing his vocal resistance, Philombe had been arrested a number of times, most recently a year or so before I was in Cameroon. The version of the story I got described how he was brought to a dank cell and held there without charges, until Ahidjo, hearing of the arrest yet never having met the writer, asked to be taken to the prison to speak with Philombe. Startled to see Philombe without

THE WORLD IS A BOOK, INDEED

the use of his legs and sitting on the floor there in the cell, Ahidjo just looked at the guards in disbelief, saying: "Is this the little man who is so dangerous to my country? Release him immediately." Of course, not even that deterred Philombe in his challenging the government, and he would be arrested again in 1981, not long after my summer there. Actually, when I was in Cameroon it took some doing, through the help of either Marcien Towa or Ernest Alima, I think, to arrange my meeting with him at his home, as Philombe's political safety understandably remained touchy.

∎

He lived in a small house, little more than a shack, painted bright aqua and on a rutted red-dirt street, dead end, or that's how I still picture it; for all intents and purposes, the house could have been the *cambuse* of his most famous book even if it wasn't the original simple habitation.

The tales (or as the French would have it, *contes*) in *Letters from My Hut* were marked by what struck me as a complex innocence. While critics noted how Philombe was influenced by his extensive reading in French literature, devouring stacks of books friends brought to his little home (surely anything from La Fontaine's animal fables to Maupassant's masterfully oblique short stories), there was a quality entirely original to that first book: it could seem naive and unschooled in its loose narrative approach, just a compilation of mere colloquial sketches, but they also had the subtle power to linger long after each was read, resonate and summon up the universal, the way any major literature does. The collection contained only nine pieces, printed with wobbly letters on rough paper in the thin original French edition published in Yaoundé.

A callow young schoolteacher dedicated to his job gets sacked for living with a prostitute in "When the Pupils' Parents Intervene." A former legendarily great beauty from a village in the bush, once the consort of African princes and lustful white colonialists, ends up ragged and selling home-brewed corn alcohol on the Yaoundé streets, though about to be evicted from her own hut she maintains an admirable dignity in "Mandari, a Fifty-Year-old Demoiselle." An abandoned kitten, "his silky white coat with mauve stripes . . . a row of milk-white chisel-like teeth," such a fragile creature, mysteriously shows up at the door of the narrator's hut one day, so gentle that it only scares away mice rather than attack them in "The Little Phantom Cat." A small neighbor boy helps the disabled narrator take care of it and attempt to nurse it back to health, and the creature becomes the narrator's welcome companion, yet like what much of life sometimes seems to add up to—only death and blank nothingness—the story ends in moving discouragement, even fear, and a moment of meditation on the biggest of all issues any of us eventually must face:

> Alas, his eyes half closed, his paws immobile and rigid, the little cat was no longer anything but a ball of cotton lying poignantly motionless in the gutter. That motionlessness which disconcerts the muse of poets, which commands respect from the genius of scholars and against which every royal scepter is powerless.

> "It was a phantom cat, sent by Providence into your hut, and it was the mice who cast an evil spell on him!" my mother said in a melancholy, superstitious voice.

> But me, I lost my good spirits and became motionless among the remains of this young companion in my solitary hours. Night fell on the city, my eyes dimmed with tears. I looked by accident at the sun which was progressively being extinguished on the uncertain horizon.

I suppose I was nervous about going to see Philombe, almost as if it were a pilgrimage. I left the tape recorder behind, because I didn't want to come across as somebody intruding on him with electronic equipment, especially considering his political difficulties, so I would only take notes.

We spoke for well over an hour in a bare front room, straw mats neatly arranged around the dirt floor. Philombe—skinny in his disability, polite and smiling, seeming shy, while his dark eyes behind oversize eyeglasses were very alive—was helped by a woman and a little girl as he got seated on a yellow wooden chair, barefoot and wearing shorts and a loose dashiki shirt. I sat across from him in another straight-back chair. The woman reappeared from the rear of the house and set down a bottle of locally brewed Guinness Stout with two glasses (there was never any shortage of beer, or sincere hospitality, for that matter, in any Cameroonian meeting), and Philombe asked me to pour a glass for each of us. The conversation was mostly in French—much of which I missed either because my French is merely functional or his was heavy with a Cameroonian inflection—and we talked the best we could about Cameroonian writing, specifically his work and the small and pretty much only publishing house in Cameroon at the time, Éditions CLÉ. A religious publisher that had widened its scope to include general poetry and fiction, CLÉ gained considerable notoriety when *Lettres de ma cambuse* on its list was honored abroad. I guess we talked about American writing, too; it was a keen interest of his, seeing as he'd visited America two years before on a three-month trip arranged by a group of U.S. African-lit scholars. He asked about my writing (I hadn't even published a first book then, just short stories in literary magazines, but a collection of them had at that very moment already been accepted by a good university press while I was away; thoroughly out of contact in those pre-email days and with long-distance calls bordering on impossible from Cameroon, I would learn the news only when my sister picked me up a few weeks later at the tiny Kingston, Rhode Island, railroad station on the Amtrak main line to take me to over to our seaside family summer place in nearby Narragansett, the train ride up from New York City being the last leg of my long trip back from Africa), and at times Philombe seemed to be deflecting any of my expressed admiration for *Letters from My Hut.* He was the kind of writer, and man, who had that quality about him, more interested in hearing about you rather than saying anything about himself and his own honored work.

In a way, such humble curiosity reminded me so of *Letters from My Hut,* where the protagonist confined to his small room looks out at those passing by outside and wonders about their lives, also wonders about the larger ways of the world in general, as said, the often baffling vagaries of human nature itself.

We sipped the warm syrupy Guinness—in Cameroon, Guinness was frequently served warm—and sometimes there was little talk, just smiling and silences, maybe a rooster whose clock was confused crowing or a motorbike repeatedly revving up outside in the street. When I left, I got up to shake his hand, thanking him again for taking the time to see me, telling him again, too, how much I enjoyed his work, which was emphatically the case.

So the interviews went well. And they did so, I suppose, granting that I wasn't a genuine scholar, never mind an Africanist, and also granting that I had no idea what in the world I would do with the material gathered here once I returned to Iowa State. I knew I had no intention of writing a book or even an article on Cameroonian literature, probably wouldn't as much as know how to go about that. Furthermore, I had no real desire, in the *least*, to become an academic scholar; the only prose I wanted to write and that occupied me more than full-time was prose fiction, meaning short stories and novels. While in Cameroon some qualms did arise every so often about this issue of my so-called research. It happened again one evening when Marcien Towa picked me up at the UNESCO compound to take me to dinner to meet with several of his fellow faculty members from the university. At the restaurant, located by a crossroads marketplace, the group of us sat on mats feasting on a huge baked river fish set on a blue platter, taking turns scooping up with our fingers the delicious flaky fare, then rinsing our hands in between courses in vinyl buckets of tap water passed around. (By this time whatever caution I had about any malady I might incur in Africa got cavalierly tossed aside, and I even was lax lately in hosing myself with insect repellent to protect against malarial mosquitoes, believing the synthetic quinine pills I gulped daily would protect me; in truth, they didn't do the job fully, and the following winter back in Iowa I suffered what was diagnosed as a belated but fortunately mild bout of the illness, first thought to be the flu.) During the meal Towa's colleagues asked me to explain to them in more detail my research, which I strained to do,

Towa graciously coming in at one point, perhaps an attempt to help me and provide his own summary:

"He's here to make us all famous!"

I sort of wished he hadn't said that.

■

I learned there was one other American in Yaoundé doing research. He was a guy on a Fulbright from a Big Ten university and teaching for a year at the University of Yaoundé. People at the club operated by the U.S. Embassy for the American diplomatic community kept telling me about him, how we should get together, though I never seemed to run into him there.

I was spending a good amount of time at the club, in fact, usually in the late afternoon after walking around for hours on end, up and down the hilly streets and into new neighborhoods thick with banana palms and breeze-rattling patches of planted sweet corn everywhere; I dodged motorbikes and growling trucks, exploring, taking it all in.

A guest membership at the club had been arranged when I first checked in with the American consular offices in the *centre-ville*, a too-obvious showcase outside the building containing photographs of successful blacks in the U.S. (an Air Force fighter-jet pilot; Muhammed Ali for some reason handing out what seemed to be an award at a Frisbee competition; etc.). There I was given a briefing on health precautions, how to receive mail (which never worked) and the like from a rugged African American guy who was quite a presence in his own right; dressed in sporty casual clothes, a big cowboy hat on his desk, he had played pro football for the Washington Redskins for a year or two, maybe the taxi squad, before entering the diplomatic corps. Possibly noticing my height, he invited me to join in on choose-up basketball sessions at the club a couple of evenings a week. I declined with some explanation how in the cold New England of my boyhood, ice hockey was the winter sport kids gravitated toward and played in school, and I was a lousy basketball player, if any sort of a basketball player at all. However,

I told him I would like to stop by the club now and then, if possible. He said he would be pleased to put my name on the list of guest members, emphasizing, "You can get a decent cheeseburger there." I took him up on the offer.

As late as then in 1979 the club remained stuck in an exaggerated time warp. While U.S. overseas involvement usually took the form of shrewd imperialism as opposed to blatant colonialism, the premises could have made an accurate set for any big-screen depiction of the relaxed tropical life of privilege in a stock movie about colonial days, even a chapter in a Somerset Maugham novel or one by that supreme colonial chronicler, the aforementioned Graham Greene. There were well-manicured grounds of lush flower gardens in loam as rich as coffee grounds and shaggy coconut palms with their trunks whitewashed lower down, some low-slung buildings for the club quarters proper. At the rear of the main club building, a long terra cotta-tile verandah with comfortably cushioned rattan chairs overlooked the tennis courts (occasionally the same young couple in whites lazily popping the ball back and forth in the stilled heat) and a small swimming pool (equally occasionally, a few little kids from diplomatic families splashing in the agate blue, or on weekends young Marines who served in the U.S. Embassy guard horsing around in the pool with teenage girls from the American International School next door). On a low ridge behind the grounds there was a high chain-link fence. Cameroonian kids would gather there to look at the scene below, as if it were a different world altogether they were watching in a film and couldn't quite believe what they saw. They probably stared not out of poverty but sheer curiosity, I'd say, because in 1979 Cameroon was a relatively economically sound sub-Saharan African country, somewhat of a success story and the population then a modest, and manageable, eight million (today about twenty-five). You encountered ragged beggars in the *centre-ville,* blind or otherwise disabled, congregating outside the monolith of the central post office the French had built back in the 1930s, but on the whole the country was reportedly doing well. Cameroon had maintained its strong agricultural base and hadn't been subject to a flight from the countryside with a discovery of abundant oil and the ensuing risk and economic fluctuation such a supposed windfall could bring, as was the situation in recently troubled Nigeria next door. It was a point of national pride among many I met that Cameroon was productive enough that it exported a considerable amount of food, a hearty surplus, to other countries. There was the unique positive spirit of the Cameroonian people figuring into this, too, and one student I spoke with at the university told me, "Even on our traditional tribal masks, look at them, there are always smiles, it is not like that in other countries. Cameroonian people are different."

On two successive Saturday nights the club offered the same film, a trucker feature, *White Line Fever*, starring Jan-Michael Vincent, and of course I passed on that.

Sometimes in the afternoon I sat out on the verandah reading, often joined by Peace Corps volunteers. The volunteers took full advantage of the club facilities whenever they came to the capital for a few days. They were usually in from the rural villages to get fresh G.G. shots, gamma globulin being not a vaccination but a necessary repeated additive to boost the blood plasma and ward off the always constant threat of hepatitis. Some stayed in the city to correct English-proficiency exams that Cameroonian students annually sat for to qualify for study in the U.S.

For a while there was a sudden larger influx of Peace Corps people from outside Cameroon, looking utterly haggard. They arrived in Yaoundé because the U.S. government had ordered their immediate evacuation from the neighboring Central African Empire. The country was ravaged under the crazed dictatorship of a certain Emperor Bokassa and currently in outright turmoil. Notorious as Uganda's Idi Amin, Bokassa was a military officer who two years prior had practically bankrupted the former French colony on his extravagant "coronation" ceremony (the jeweled crown alone cost an estimated five million dollars); the previous April, observing from maybe his palace window that schoolchildren were demonstrating against purchasing the blue-and-white uniforms he'd mandated for all schoolchildren (his wife owned the company that sold them), he soon dispatched armed soldiers from his Imperial Guard to punish the protestors, a bloody massacre ensuing and an estimated one hundred killed. I found it strange, or eerily ominous, to hear the Peace Corps kids talking about "The Empire" in their conversation, the usual two-word appellation for the country being what they routinely used in chatting and the "Central African" part of the formal name always left out.

In the dim, small bar off the club restaurant—empty one weekday afternoon, the ceiling fan chugging—I was having that American-style cheeseburger the consular officer recommended, pretty good and doused with authentic Heinz ketchup, and I finally met the other researcher, the guy from the Big Ten university. It took less than five minutes of conversation for both of us to be *amazed* that here we were in Central Africa, most likely the sole outside researchers on the culture of this particular country halfway around the world at this particular moment, and as it turned out, we—almost the exact same age, too—had grown up in adjoining towns in Rhode Island and only several miles apart. Before long we were bouncing around names of friends we might have in common or cousins who had gone to the other's high school, that sort of thing; we even joked about a barbershop we both went to as kids. He was wiry and pale with a faint ginger mustache and sloppy summer clothes, had the voice of a born wise guy. He said I should stop by his apartment some afternoon for more talk, also to get a better idea of what it was like being an expat living in Yaoundé, if only a temporary one like him on his one-year Fulbright teaching appointment.

I had a hard time finding the apartment in another hilly district, a recently developed quarter I wasn't familiar with. The modern poured-concrete complex was studded with stacked, overhanging poured-concrete balconies, the whole package looking oddly top-heavy (sometimes you got the feeling that Yaoundé served as one extended test ground for wackily far-out French architecture that France itself wasn't exactly ready for). The complex might have been planned as more or less luxury accommodation, but, still rather new, was already run-down, an unkempt courtyard of broken tiles and the empty ornamental pool there dusty and now more a depository for piled garbage than anything else. Up in the sparsely furnished two-room flat with a linoleum floor and blank walls opening out to the balcony, we sat and sipped a couple of smaller bottles of cold "33" beer (not the warm Guinness; he admitted how he himself hadn't gotten used to that temperature for beer), and at first as we talked he said nothing about the Cameroonian girl quietly sitting in the one easy chair by the balcony reading a magazine. In white shorts and an orange tube top, her smile emphasizing deep dimples and hair fashionably short-cropped, giant eyes, she was slight, delicate-featured, and very pretty. After he eventually explained she was his "girlfriend," adding she was quite shy and without any English, only Ewondo and some French, he called over to her in French something along the lines of, "You are shy, isn't that true, chérie?" To which she just raised those big eyes and smilingly nodded to him, then, saying nothing, went back to slowly flipping through the glossy photos in the magazine—a thick copy of *Playboy*. Honestly. The guy from the Big Ten university told me his subscription got forwarded to him here with the rest of his mail from home, and he said she loved to look at the pictures whenever a new issue arrived. He next said to her in French something along the lines of, "You like those pictures, don't you, chérie?" to which she only smiled again, softly giggled, too, with dimples really showing as she didn't look up from her intent gazing at the pages.

■

No need to rehash our goofing around with more talk of Rhode Island, but I did find his story of the route that had brought him to Cameroon definitely interesting. His field, and the subject of his PhD, was African American studies, not African studies. However, he said that as a white in that field his credibility might not be entirely solid, a looming danger in light of the fact he was coming up for tenure soon. The university in Yaoundé was interested in African American studies, possibly had wanted an American to teach courses in the literature, from the classics of the Harlem Renaissance right up to the searing autobiographies of Eldridge Cleaver and Malcom X, so they arranged for a Fulbright position. He told me that he saw the opening advertised and knew that living in Africa for a year and looking into African culture while there might provide the edge he needed, a valuable plus, when an always tricky tenure vote came up—or one *very* tricky in his case, he repeated, because he was, well, *white*. I listened to his story, and he next launched into generalized beefing, with little appreciation of what to me appeared to be his enviably easy life in Cameroon, a place that I personally was finding wonderful—my excitement of being there one day was only surpassed by the excitement of being there the next, though I realized a year-long stay this distant from home might be altogether different. The snideness in his voice got summoned in full:

"I've put up with a whole lot here for almost a year now, roasting my ass off in this non-stop heat and also holding back on complaining about the bullshit at the university, which is basically all total confusion. Still, I can say that I'll be able to bank close to thirty thousand bucks, the way it turns out, with my expenses paid here by the Fulbright thing and my university at home having given me a year paid sabbatical to overlap with that."

He said he was going to buy a Porsche with the money he'd made on the deal once he got back, because that's what he had wanted for a long time now, a new Porsche 911 coupe; he deserved it after a year in Africa, he pronounced.

He continued on with more talk about his displeasure with the inefficiency of nearly everything at the university. I countered with how graciously I had been treated by Marcien Towa and his colleagues there. I also pointed out how there were many things about the university itself—where I'd been using the library to track down books—I found fascinating. Strolling around the campus of scattered mismatching buildings, I'd been impressed by the seriousness with which education seemed to be approached. One day I noticed in the central mall of burnt yellow grass and huge, spreading-limb shade trees how long white pages with students' course grades were tacked onto the tree trunks for everybody to see; there was no hemming and hawing about privacy or hurting anybody's feelings as in the U.S., where student transcripts—as far as any school administration was concerned—could be as guarded as any top-secret formula for nuclear fusion. Better, I spotted on another day a number of students, boys, trying to boost each other up to the high open windows of a packed-to-capacity lecture hall, one on top of another in what looked like a shaky cheerleaders' pyramid, so they could listen to the lecture underway. It was good indication of how hungry for education young people were in a society where I'd heard that sometimes an entire rural village financed your travel to study in the capital and contributed to buying your books.

"I did have one snag over there," I admitted to the guy, slowly sipping his beer now.

"What was that?"

He snickered some, one eyebrow arching and the scraggly ginger mustache that hadn't grown in quite right making him look more the wise guy than ever. I detected he was taking satisfaction in catching me in a bit of my own dissatisfaction, if only to confirm his aggravation and extensive griping.

I told him how I finally had gone to introduce myself to the head of the literature department. He was a pompous man, hefty and loud-bellowing, who wore an expensive French-cut suit and a sort of Carnaby Street wide, floral-print tie at a shirt collar too tight around his rolled-fat neck, some glitzy gold rings on his fingers to boot and the get-up overall certainly not the expected academic's attire. Apparently, he had already seen me around the campus, gotten word about me.

"He wasn't very pleasant," I said. "And sitting behind his desk there, he looked at me in my shirtsleeves and told me never to show up on campus without wearing a suit jacket. He said a professor should look like a professor, that was important. Also, when I mentioned to him that I had eaten in the student refectory, he absolutely disapproved of that, and he stressed I should never, above all, be seen eating with students: professors just didn't do that. I guess it's due to the old French system that education is based on here, rigid, and the pecking order is established."

"See?" he said.

"What?" I asked.

"That's exactly the kind of thing I'm talking about, the bullshit. The man's a complete phony, and it has nothing to do with any rigid French system. He claims he has a PhD from some place in the U.K., Leeds, maybe, while most everybody suspects it's only a tall tale and has little truth to it other than the fact he lived in England for a while, probably did some graduate study there but never got any formal PhD. He's a load of hot air. But nobody is so crazy as to question him on it, and that would be the last thing anybody in their right mind would want to do, because his brother is a big-time general, a member of the government in-crowd and tight with the illustrious Cameroonian president himself, Ahidjo. No, when it comes to that character, believe me, you are *never* to ask him about his degree."

Which, in fact, could have been the case, as others later confirmed.

If nothing else, hearing the guy from the Big Ten university go on that afternoon as his girlfriend leisurely enjoyed the fleshy, studio-lit centerfold and such, I knew that at least I had run into somebody who seemed engaged in a genuine ruse in academia, much more byzantine and even duplicitous than my simply having found my own roundabout way to fund a trip to the continent, the home of the literature I'd been fervently reading. And, to jump ahead some, any lingering guilt concerning that was nicely erased when I moved on to a job at the University of Texas a year later. On the faculty at Texas was a very respected Africanist, Bernth ("Ben") Lindfors, and one afternoon he told me that a fellow Africanist would be visiting Austin for a few days, Richard Bjornson of Ohio State University, another Big Ten school. An authority on French Cameroonian literature, Bjornson was the English translator of René Philombe's writing, and he was working on a long, comprehensive history of the country's literature. Ben knew I had the interview material, and he said that Bjornson would be pleased to receive it, as I suggested. The interviews had been transcribed from the tapes on a huge, loud-clacking IBM Selectric typewriter set up in my campus office at Iowa State by a diligent work-study student, her assistance part of the grant package; a thick sheaf of pages had resulted but currently they were stuffed and left lying dormant in the bottom drawer of a gray metal filing cabinet in my Texas office. I did meet and speak with Bjornson in a small nook of a bar, the Cactus Café, in the university's student union, and he told me he couldn't wait to see what I had, which I assured him I'd send him once he returned to Columbus—it was good to eventually know that there might actually be *some use* for it. Anyway, that afternoon in Cameroon with the guy from the Big Ten university, I think he suggested we get together again, but by that point I really didn't need another dose of his company, or more so, his outlook.

And, besides, my stay was rapidly drawing to a close.

■

Done with my interviewing work in Yaoundé, I spent a week traveling around the western sector of the country, the former British colony where English was spoken. That made for a good little education in itself concerning the difference in the lingering effects of former colonization; for instance, the old Anglophone presence meant eggs and cornflakes for breakfast, plus tea, naturally, and not the usual strong coffee with rolls and jam of the more "continental" fare consumed at the start of the day in French-speaking Yaoundé.

In Victoria, a town at the foot of Mount Cameroon in the western Anglophone sector, I booked into an older hotel, formerly a British hospital and right on the Atlantic. Usually listed as one of the wettest places on earth, Victoria had an average annual rainfall of about thirty-five feet. The dark clouds rolled in from the open ocean and the first resistance they hit was the massive single mountain, unloading continuously. People in the streets wore rubber sandals and a minimum of thin, easily dryable clothes, accustomed to getting soaked; I once saw a guy outside a shop repeatedly trying to light a soggy cigarette with flickering matches that repeatedly went out in the wet, but he kept at it, determined. In the warm tropical rain I swam alone at the hotel's deserted gray beach, making sure to stay within the limits of the shark nets marked by bobbing yellow floats, as the hotel clerk had prudently advised me. I next took a packed, wildly painted van of the sort generically called a "mammy wagon" (the term came from the fact that market women often used them) along the corkscrewing cliffside road to the old German capital of Buea, alluded to earlier, high up on Mount Cameroon. The ascent of the near perpendicular-steep mountain was bumpy yet enjoyable, offering prime vistas around every tight curve, though the next day the trip back down became as wild as a carnival ride. The hip young driver wore a newsboy cap atop his perfectly spherical puff of hair and had the van's dash converted into all but an altar in honor of Bob Marley—photos of the reggae star plastering it—and he didn't seem to pay much attention to the brake pedal whatsoever (I later learned the drivers got paid by the number of runs they could make each day); one of a trio of African women with me in back politely regurgitated into an empty red cocoa tin the whole ride (a common practice due to local people often not being used to motor travel and suffering motion sickness, I also later learned, the maneuver performed quite gracefully). After that I took a bus back to Cameroon's other large city, Francophone Doula on the coast, now getting to know it some, too, the neighborhoods and even its oddities.

As can happen on a second time around, the place took on a fuller and much different character, needless to add, than on that first night there and what now felt like many years, not a month and a half or so, since I had to parry with the young hooker to retrieve the room key, my having been pretty disoriented then upon first arrival, if not totally lost. In Doula there were sizable lizards, translucently orange and black, noisily swishing through the trees and shrubbery beside the sidewalks, something you got used to. In the middle of the city there was a modern road ramp on pillars for what looked like the start of a sleek, elevated multilane freeway that suddenly ended in mid-air, water ski-jump fashion, baffling. I wondered if the project had been funded by either the Americans or the Soviets, which many such projects were during the ongoing Cold War, Ernest Alima had told me, the two superpowers vying for influence in Africa, but in this case the funding perhaps having been yanked mid-project without any explanation, as could also happen, it seemed.

My Pan Am overseas flight to the U.S. would leave from Senegal. I purposefully booked what was somewhat of a milk train on Nigerian Airways from Doula to Dakar. The early-model, sloppily refurbished old 707 (on the cabin's light-green trim within, you could see brush marks from repainting by hand) made extended stops in a list of countries, sometimes for hours because of the compounding delays. The layovers were enough to have a couple of relaxed beers in the usually small, single-building airports with mosquito-infested waiting rooms—Lagos in Nigeria, Lomé in Togo, Abidjan in Côte d'Ivoire, and Freetown in Sierra Leone—before finally arriving in Senegal. Dakar was definitely a Muslim city, loudspeakers rigged with exposed wiring on the ancient, intricately architected mosques calling out prayers. The tall Senegalese, both men and women, were known for their handsomeness, immediately obvious, and it was also easy to understand how the French colonizers considered Dakar their jewel in sub-Saharan Africa. There were Gallic outdoor cafés and sweeping golden beaches; why, the French had founded their most respected university in sub-Saharan Africa there, which remained a center of intellectual life in Africa.

One brilliant, gull-squealing day I took a boat ride from Dakar out to Gorée Island. Gorée was a beautiful spot if you could manage to forget for a few minutes, while strolling among the ruins of the imposing semicircular stone fortress and grim iron-barred cells, that this was once the infamous Isle of Slaves, the central deportation center on the continent for human beings in chains to be shipped across the Atlantic for a steady supply of forced labor. I'd gotten to talking with a French tourist on the boat and we strolled around Gorée together for a couple of hours. While we waited for the return boat, he snapped my photo using the small 35-mm camera I'd brought, the sole picture of me from the trip. I seldom used the camera, always suspicious that to rely on photos would be to run the risk of sacrificing the intensity of any scene while it's actually happening. Slim, dark-haired, mustached, and tanned, I appear rather swashbuckling in an open-collar blue chambray work shirt and gray corduroy jeans, a red day pack over one shoulder while standing in front of a thatch-roof bar beside the docks (the wreck I behold in the glaring silver mirror each morning now in what has turned out to be 2018 tells a rockier tale, of course), and it's tough to believe that anybody, let alone me, was ever *that* young.

Having operated well within my grant budget so far, I'd decided to splurge a bit in Dakar, and there were extra funds now to spread around. I was staying in a genuinely four-star hotel, in truth not all that expensive and futuristic in design—streamlined, plenty of of glass—right on the city's shimmering aqua bay and, as it turned out, with a view of the white wedding-cake rise of the Presidential Palace surrounded by tall palms on the opposite shore.

Every night while in Dakar I went out on the hotel's long walkway, my hands planted on the ship-style pipe railing, and I looked across the water—now stilled and glassy black—to the palace; it rose very white, those palm trees around it dark silhouettes. The nation's head of state lived there, I knew, yet the attraction for me—more significantly and even quite startlingly—was that the Senegalese president, Léopold Senghor, was also one of the most accomplished poets worldwide in the twentieth century, a surrealist master. He'd left Senegal when young to be educated at the prestigious École Normale Supérieure in Paris and was an intellectual compatriot of Sartre and the Caribbean writers Aimé Césaire and Léon Damas there; together with Césaire and Damas in Paris, he launched the Négritude cultural movement in the 1930s, the foundation of modern Francophone African and Caribbean literature. Back in Senegal after fighting with the French Resistance in World War II (he was captured by the Germans), he became increasingly active in national politics, though that probably was always secondary to his true calling as a poet and cultural theorist. A book I'd read over and over before traveling was a selection of his poems, *Nocturnes,* number 71 in the Heinemann African Writers Series, a favorite text in many college courses in African literature, apparently.

So, the last night in Dakar, the stubs of my elongated, stapled green-and-white return ticket (remember those?) checked a half-dozen times and my vinyl flight bag packed and the many pockets tightly zipped and bulging with more books I'd acquired in both Cameroon and now Senegal along with gifts for family and friends (at a busy street marketplace in

Dakar, I bought everybody either wooden salad utensils supposed to look like carved black ebony or dashiki shirts, the latter a sure-fire hit, I hoped, a royal-blue one with particularly intricate white embroidery trimming the collar for a girl I was currently pursuing in Iowa), yes, I was out the walkway again on my last night, a perfect way to wrap up my literary travel. I liked to think how possibly Senghor was asleep and dreaming right then in the palace, generating that way, in his own meandering slumber, more and more of his hauntingly surreal verses. And maybe simply the thought of dreaming seemed to echo how my own time in Africa—which was beyond startling in its richness of sights and people and sheer unexpected happenings, also my learning more about that literature I loved—it all somehow took on the quality of a fine dream as well, and even today it can feel very much so when I do look back.

I mean, did I really find myself shaking the bony hand of a soft-spoken crippled man, a very brave writer who had survived repeated arrests for his beliefs, in a dim room and as a rooster garglingly crowed outside, or did that never happen and I just dreamed it a few nights ago? And did I really sit in a stark apartment thousands of miles from home with another guy I'd met only by chance and chat about our native Rhode Island while his pretty African girlfriend relaxed in an easy chair and smilingly flipped through a copy of *Playboy*, or did I just dream that, too, maybe last night here in Austin where I live? And, strangest of very strange scenes, did I *really* watch those boys at the university hoisting each other up as if a troupe of clowning acrobats, determined to listen in on a lecture at a ramshackle university, or was that yet another nighttime imagining in the course of my writing this, and surely dreams should always have their happy measure of comedy, no? Indeed, any one of those moments could have been a scenario in a dream, and as many who have spent time on the continent have written, some of them seasoned in world exploration, Africa can do that to you, possibly to a greater degree than any other place where you might have been the traveler, especially when wandering solo on a trip.

Actually, rather than attempt to describe my last night while I stood there and gazed at the palace, it might be better to simply offer a sample of the poetry of the man himself in conclusion, how Senghor could capture that certain dreamlike feeling I'm groping for now—a metaphysical essence—as he beautifully does capture it in a few lines from his well-known poem "Night in Sine":

Now the stars appear and the Night dreams,
Leaning on that hill of clouds, dressed in its long, milky pagne . . .
The roofs of the huts shine tenderly.
What are they saying so secretly to the stars?

■

Yes, honorary Africanist that I was lucky enough to have been at least for a while way back in 1979, and remembering and reconstructing that time in my life the best I can here as I write this today, still such an admirer of the continent's literature, I'll defer to the magic of the true poet on that.

Wholeheartedly and without any question whatsoever.

—*Antioch Review,* 2018

Postscript: Recently, since this essay first appeared in a magazine, international news reported that what had been escalating in the past several years, tensions between the Anglophone and Francophone sectors of Cameroon, had finally led to a period of extreme violence. For me that meant a certain sadness to think again of the admirable progress there had once been in the country, which, when I visited in 1979, seemed a model of general success after independence, a working example for those throughout Africa who at the time aspired to true Pan-Africanism and eventual united goals on the continent despite ethnic or other cultural differences.

To Read a Continent

Reviewing Boetie, Updike, Coetzee, Naipaul, and Gordimer; Plus a Poem, "African Airports"

BOOK REVIEW ASSIGNMENT EDITORS tend to be a harried lot, understandably. They like to categorize those in their reviewing stable for quick and very ready reference, or they used to do so when actual book reviewing was a thriving activity back in the days of flick-flicking desk Rolodexes, let's say.

Any shred of alleged expertise can be valued: this writer knows something about horse racing, this one knows something about Asian cooking, this one knows an awful lot about FDR. Aware of my keen interest in Africa, especially after my trip to interview writers in Cameroon in 1979, editors of journals and magazines often assigned me books to review from or about Africa. It meant that I found myself in a fortunate position to keep up with the literature well after my time traveling there in 1979.

For a while I was a regular reviewer of fiction for the Jesuit weekly *America*, and sometimes books set in Africa came my way from their offices in midtown Manhattan. At the time *America* operated a thriving general-interest (surely not strictly religious) book section, and it was quite common to pick up a novel in a bookstore and see a quote from a review in *America* prominently displayed on the cover, a trusted source; among the better-known past contributors to the magazine was Flannery O'Connor. I also wrote a number of reviews for *Africa Today*, my association with that journal going back to the reconsideration piece on Dugmore Boetie's nightmarish novel *Familiarity Is the Kingdom of the Lost*, mentioned already in these pages.

What follows are some of those reviews, a selection of them and together a composite essay in a way, to provide discussion of a personal recommended reading list of books about the continent.

Reviews are what they are, usually not intended to last. Even when it comes to the work of skilled and prolific reviewers who qualify as major creative artists in their own right—Joyce Carol Oates and John Updike, for example—their book-length collections of reviews, as undeniably strong as the work is, obviously aren't supposed to hold up as well as their dazzling fiction over time. Which makes sense, because a review is more or less by definition news, a blaring trumpet call on pulpy pages— or, again, it used to be like that, anyway—from a hopefully well-chosen, knowledgeable, and engaging commentator to offer a meaningful discussion of a new release. (Sadly, we're living in a time when the whole understanding of what constitutes a professional book review appears to be rapidly evanescing. Hard-copy space for reviews in magazines and particularly Sunday newspapers is, in fact, shrinking to near invisibility, going the way of that ancient Rolodex, and the online customer opinion appears to be taking over. Whether beefing or celebrating, the latter accompanied by a string of classroom-style gold stars, the customer opinion of a book does sometimes get labeled as—quite mistakenly, I think—an actual "review" on sites like Amazon and the social-media-oriented Goodreads, which is owned by conglomerative Amazon and where people often affix funny avatars, including the inevitable one I noticed the other day that showed the photo of a plump calico cat wearing a tiny beret and apparently seriously engulfed in reading a large open book. While the spiritedness of customer opinion is appreciated, even the honesty, for better or worse, of those opinions—which can be refreshing amid the outright puffery often surrounding the legitimate media reviews lately that sometimes seem mere extensions of a publisher's publicity machine—nobody really expects—or gets—much more overall literary expertise from a customer opinion than when the same customer who wrote that opinion clicks to another site and offers his or her views on the performance of a homeowner's mini-chainsaw or the comfort of a pair of memory-foam sneakers; also, when you read an entry where "author" is spelled "arthur," it doesn't exactly shout critical prowess). Not that now and then there haven't been practitioners who have made mainstream book reviewing a devoted, full-time calling, producing work that does last and can rise to the level of true art. To name a couple of them as examples, there's Britisher Cyril Connolly, the elegant and intellectually ruminating regular book columnist for the *Observer* and then the *Sunday Times* of London in the mid-twentieth century, as well as—uncannily insightful in his intimate prose, so much sheer voice to the writing—Sven Birkerts, who currently edits the respected literary magazine *Agni* at Boston University and has for forty years contributed outstanding literary criticism to many large-circulation outlets—*Esquire*, *The Atlantic*, the *New York Review of Books*, and others.

All of which is to say, in offering a selection of my reviews of books by African writers or about Africa here, I know that when writing on each, I hoped, if nothing else, it would primarily provide a valid appraisal of a book upon its release. I personally have never seen reviewing as an opportunity to exhibit one's own verbal flash, but rather it's a straightforward contract to *tell* about the book, one way or another and as honestly as possible. Nevertheless, the reviews I've selected for assembly here (including the one reconsideration) deal with work I still admire, my having reread each book again long after the review appeared, and, true, all the books are most highly—even outright emphatically—recommended.

Besides the piece that takes a second look at Boetie's novel, there are reviews of work by two other modern writers from South Africa, both internationally celebrated: J. M. Coetzee and Nadine Gordimer. With Coetzee's *Waiting for the Barbarians*, it was my second time writing on him, and I believe I hold the nice distinction of being the very first in the United States to review this eventual Nobel Prize winner (I later met him and he personally confirmed it) when his first novel—the not very well-known *Dusklands*, published by the small South African house Ravan—was assigned to me by *Africa Today*. My comment on Gordimer was delivered in a compound, two-book review that maybe yields a larger conclusion, which one does aim for with such a combination piece, in this case written for the opinion magazine *The Progressive*. The review posits Gordimer's novel envisioning a dystopic postapartheid South Africa, *July's People*, alongside a particularly thorough documentation of how that country's media was frustratedly handcuffed at the height of strict enforcement of the policy that separated races—*Up Against Apartheid*, by a former editor at *Newsweek* and *The Nation*, Richard Pollak. Actually, during the stretch when I did most of this reviewing related to Africa, the late 1970s and early 1980s, the assignments frequently were books specifically from South Africa. South Africa was always in the news at the time, and taking a stand against the injustice of apartheid had become nothing short of a worldwide movement by then, something that review assignment editors would adopt as a loud, emphatic cause of their own as well. Though politics have indeed changed dramatically in South Africa since the publication of these books about the country, I believe they possess continuing relevance as both reliable documentation of the strange era, which should not be forgotten, and an especially apt warning today of what can happen when we let ingrained irrational hate block out better judgment and basic human concern.

Two writers from outside Africa I reviewed wrote telling novels growing out of time they spent on the continent. There's John Updike, a wielder of jeweled prose who apparently based his book *The Coup* on material gathered when he made a hop-scotching U.S. government-sponsored lecture tour of several sub-Saharan countries with his wife in 1973; and there's V. S. Naipaul, an always restless traveler whose various journeys of geopolitical investigation have also yielded much subsequent significant fiction. Bound galleys of Naipaul's novel, *A Bend in the River,* were sent to me by *America* in the usual padded brown envelope, arriving only a few days after my return from Africa (how good it always was to receive a new book, usually accompanied by a typed or scribbled couple of lines on a letterhead slip tucked in the pages, giving a due date for the review and the number of words, the ground rules of the trade; you always had to be careful not to prick your finger on the padded envelope's staples when you tore it open to see—or, more exactly, *discover*—what was inside); moved and surely still excited by my firsthand experience following my trip then in 1979, I took issue with Naipaul's pessimistic portrait of Africa, a judgment I've since pulled back on, I must admit. *A Bend in the River* exudes dark anxiety bordering on existential dread, delivered with intense evocations of place and subtly revealing dialogue. The model for the novel's unnamed country is the Democratic Republic of the Congo, formerly Zaire and the territory of Conrad's *Heart of Darkness* as well as, when Naipaul visited, an oppressive ruler who attempted to have himself declared President for Life, Mobuto Sese Seko of the dark sunglasses and trademark leopard-skin hats along with such exquisitely tailored, African-cut sharkskin suits; called the "Big Man" in Naipaul's novel, Mobutu was a confirmed tyrant who developed a strong cult of personality, a figure no less crazed than the more flamboyantly bespangled Emperor Jean-Bédel Bokassa himself, who actually wore a jewel-studded crown and operated at the time over in the Central African Empire. For me, with that stay just the summer before in Cameroon—a country in 1979 still enjoying to a degree the spirit of optimism that spread throughout Africa after the first wave of independence in the 1960s and that lingered well into the 1970s—Naipaul's grim conclusions seemed small, even mean-spirited. But, as said, I came to later recognize how undeniably prescient he was in warning what could happen—and in some countries was already beginning to happen—when much of the upbeat celebratory hope in these new African nations increasingly gave way to major disorder and a continent largely ravaged for over twenty-five years by wars and rampant corruption almost beyond belief, even mass genocide (Rwanda-Burundi the most tragic story on that count), with trouble spots remaining today (South Sudan, Somalia, and the Congo).

In rereading this work I notice in my observations how the very dreamlike quality that has characterized Africa for both me and others does emerge as a recurring motif, whether in an author's exploring it via a mythic approach, as in Updike, or its expressing the unreality of life becoming an unsettling nightmare, as in the apartheid-haunted South African writers (foremost Boetie) whose books I wrote on.

I've also tacked on here a poem of my own, hopefully not too presumptuously, "African Airports." It isn't any accurate record of my own travel, though maybe calls to mind the essential tenor of such travel in general. Also, for purposes of its serving as an addendum to my essay in this collection "Honorary Africanist," which deals directly with my time in Cameroon, the poem might provide a brief sample of the creative writing and actual product—mostly short stories and some poems, too—

that grew out of that stay in Africa. Ben Lindfors, the respected, very well-known Africanist at the University of Texas where I teach, once told me that he'd made a copy of the poem from the literary magazine in which it appeared and had it mounted and framed, to hang in his bedroom at home. The magazine, *William and Mary Review*, illustrated the poem with an etching of a giraffe, and I guess it suggested Africa, an easy symbol; while said graceful, long-necked wild animal had nothing whatsoever to do with the work, it added visual artistic flare to the two-page spread that Ben had framed.

I can be frank (sane?) in saying I'm pretty sure I've never written *any* poem that deserves to be mounted and framed anywhere. But with that gesture coming from somebody like Ben, a generous man who dedicated his career to the literature of Africa (he constantly took up the cause of African writers, often broke, when he knew they could use help landing a visiting teaching slot at a university in the U.S.; there were always wonderful reception parties for any African writer passing through Austin at the rambling old wood-frame house of Ben and his wife Judy near campus, with faculty, students, and the African writer happily mixing and the talk probably some of the best in all my years at the university; he recently donated his entire library of thousands of books from or about Africa to a university in South Africa), true, merely Ben's approving of my poem with an African subject, never mind framing it, meant a good deal to me.

As did just the opportunity to write these reviews of such solid books about Africa when younger, assigned by those harried editors who always so kindly kept me in mind.

A Reconsideration of *Familiarity Is the Kingdom of the Lost: The Story of a Black Man in South Africa*, by Dugmore Boetie

In the midst of all the television reports and newspaper stories in the past year about racial confrontations in South Africa, I found myself turning to books I had read by writers from that country. What first came to mind was that of a South African black—Dugmore Boetie's *Familiarity Is the Kingdom of the Lost*. In fact, I realized I wanted to reread it before going back to some of the better-known South African writing in English.

Familiarity Is the Kingdom of the Lost originally appeared in England after Boetie's death in 1966. It was issued later in the U.S. as a hardbound and subsequently a Fawcett paperback. Barney Simon, a white South African playwright and publisher, believed in Boetie's innate writing ability and was the editor for the author's rough manuscript. In an afterword, Simon explains how he gave money and raised more from his own friends to allow Boetie, sick and testy, to leave his Johannesburg factory job and write the "true" story of his checkered life in South African slums, the segregated townships of the big cities. As it turned out, the factual truth didn't interest Boetie, despite Simon's pleas for it.

Boetie exaggerated enormously. The result is a bragging first-person narrative of the often absurdly far-fetched exploits of a one-legged, streetwise petty thief named Dugmore Boetie trying to survive in the 1930s through '50s. It is therefore not really an autobiography because of that exaggeration, and not really a novel because of its basis in the facts of Boetie's life. The book in the Fawcett edition bears the simple subtitle, rather noncommittal, "The Story of a Black Man in South Africa."

Novelist Nadine Gordimer visited Boetie several times in a Johannesburg hospital before he died. Prefacing the Fawcett edition, she praises Simon for his kindness and patience in dealing with Boetie and says that Simon "Asked him [Boetie] for his confidence and received deception. Asked for the truth and received lies. How could it have been otherwise, if Dugmore Boetie were to remain true to himself? What should he know of gratitude, the South African black who must take off his hat and say Thank you, *baas*, not for what comes to him as a right—for nothing comes to him as a right—but for the tithe of the white man's abundance handed out at the back door?"

However, once you start reading, you soon realize that the exaggeration evokes a dreamlike atmosphere, which in a way must accurately portray the essential feeling of what life *is* like for so many blacks in the bleak South African slums. There, the odds against a normal existence continue to be so stacked that existence itself must seem routinely unbelievable. In short, Boetie's inability to stick to the facts paradoxically results in an alternatingly comic and horrifying picaresque odyssey of deeper insight.

Dugmore—the formal first name came from Duggie, which in turn was the name of an elephant whose feet he washed on a circus job—drifts in and out of gangs and louse-infested prisons. He steals with dash, cons drinks, looks for work only occasionally because work is never available, suffers brutality in enormous doses and inflicts it likewise. A good sample of the writing's tenor is the opening scene. His mother beats him as a child with a strap and then a frying pan to make him say the word "Mother." He reacts: "I pushed and her skinny body fell into the greedy flames of a healthy fire-galley. Maybe I had broken her back, or maybe she was just too exhausted to lift herself. Anyway, my mother just fried and fried. . . ." The story may ramble, but an ability to write clear, painfully precise description shouldn't be overlooked: "The streets were muddy and slimy because they were without gutters. They were strewn with dirty dishwater. The air reeked of overflowing latrines. Naked children with bloated bellies stood lined up, staring at us with mouths hanging open. . . ."

Rereading this book reaffirmed my belief in the paramount importance of books in a society such as ours—one that can rely too heavily on the noisy, more popular mass media—when it comes to understanding political issues abroad. So, I don't limit that importance to only nonfiction books which directly address themselves to politics. Boetie's penetrating prose gives a sense of the stakes involved in South Africa, a sense of the people. And it is an element that brief newspaper and television attention usually fails to convey. Even the so-called in-depth analyses fall short.

In this writing there are no hidden solutions to apply to the turbulence that now rages in South Africa, though if a solution hopefully does materialize the media will report the news of it effectively. Meanwhile Boetie doesn't report. He tells us, mysteriously whispers to us, something very powerful indeed.

—*Africa Today*, 1978

The Coup, by John Updike

John Updike has written a novel about a black dictator named Elleloû in an imaginary contemporary upper-African state called Kush, which penetrates the Sahara in the north and is fertile enough for peanut production in the south.

Now it may seem strange that Updike has turned to such an alien setting when the bulk of his fiction has been set in the small-town Pennsylvania of his youth and the suburban New England of his adulthood. But Updike traveled throughout Africa as a Fulbright lecturer in 1973, and his obvious enthusiasm for literature from that continent is attested to by how much criticism about it he has contributed to *The New Yorker* over the years.

Elleloû (the concocted name supposedly means "freedom") grew up in Kush when it was a French colony and still known as Noire, studied at a small private college in bucolic Wisconsin, and returned to his homeland to take over the government in the name of revolutionary socialism. When the story begins in 1973, a sensitive, cynical President Elleloû (who narrates in the first person, though he often refers to himself in the imperial third) realizes that he is losing his power as a drought plagues the country, leaving the people restless and his untrustworthy lieutenants very itchy for upheaval. The main lines of narration deal with the building governmental imbroglio, Elleloû's own search to find himself, and the tales of his earlier life with his four wives. The wives range from a hefty Kush woman of his village to a complaining white Wisconsin girl he met in college, who comes to his country only to miss the conveniences of America and be absolutely miserable.

It all works wonderfully well. Updike has hit upon an effective semicomic tone. Such lightheartedness may preclude this from becoming a major statement on the Third World (a surely sober subject) but it also ensures against it degenerating to dull sermonizing, which has been the downfall of too much literature setting out to make such a major statement. There are, the semicomic tone notwithstanding, substantial measures of genuinely insightful cultural and political observation here.

There are fine mythic echoes, too. In one sequence, Elleloû ventures into the desert in search of the severed head of the ex-king, a father figure whom he ordered decapitated. The head reportedly is spouting invective against Elleloû from a cave in the barren northern regions. There are haunting passages recounting dreams, thoughtful reflections on the Koran, touching exchanges between Elleloû and those wives, and a packed-to-capacity crowd of intriguing minor characters.

And there is Updike's rare gift of language. An Updike sentence has always been easily identifiable by its poetic flare—a combination of full vocabulary and intense sensuality. It seems to me that the vividness of the African scene is made for these sentences, maybe as the vividness of the South Seas was made for Gaugin's canvases. As a quick example, here is Updike describing a desert caravan: "We were awakened beneath the stars—the stars! in the midnight absolute that arched above Balak the constellations hung inflamed like chandeliers—and we made our way, tinkling and sighing and snorting, toward the pearl dawn whose blush was as delicate as the pink tinge of nacre, to that point in mid-morning when the camels began to squat down simply of despair."

Updike has previously made brief excursions away from his standard domestic settings, in some of his short stories, for instance, and in his linked collection *Bech: A Book,* which brings a traveling American writer to Eastern Bloc communist countries. But with *The Coup* he has gambled in taking on the African setting so wholeheartedly in the person of a contemplative revolutionary dictator. The gamble has paid off, proving Updike's versatility beyond denial. It may be that such versatility is what will keep this major American novelist ranked as just that for many, many years to come.

—*America Magazine,* 1978

Waiting for the Barbarians, by J. M. Coetzee

Readers will recognize that the title of this new novel by South African J. M. Coetzee is taken from that of a poem by Constantine Cavafy, who wrote in Greek and died in his native Egypt in 1933. Such borrowing seems appropriate, because in careful language and narrative intensity, this slim book does read very much like a poem.

Coetzee sets his tale in the harsh, semiarid frontier of a major power called the Empire. An aging man in charge of a settlement there, the Magistrate, is content to live out his days quietly, administering over the small community, visiting a gentle prostitute at the local inn, and collecting anthropological artifacts in casual excavations manned by his soldiers. But Colonel Joll from the Empire's Third Bureau of the Civil Guard arrives for an investigation of supposed plotting among the "barbarians," peaceful indigenous tribes who dwell beyond the settlement. Joll brutally interrogates barbarians taken as prisoners; eventually, a beaten boy gives him a story that his people are organizing for war, the child fabricating the information obviously out of sheer fear. Joll leaves and the prisoners are released to go off on their own, all except for a young barbarian woman who is left behind, half blind and with near-crippled bloody feet, another victim of Joll's cruel interrogations. The compassionate Magistrate develops a strange fascination with her and brings her into his own chamber, as he bathes and oils her feet nightly in a ritual of sorts and nurses her back to health. When he sets out on an expedition across the frozen, treacherous outlying wastes in March to return her to her people, and when the Empire, acting on Joll's findings, launches a military campaign against the barbarians and dispatches a dashing young officer in a lilac-blue uniform named Mandel to take over the Magistrate's outpost, the Magistrate is charged with consorting with the enemy. His agonizing but defiant downfall follows, in a long series of humiliations and tortures.

This is an extremely powerful and intoxicating piece of writing, haunted by Kafka, with the creation of a mythic setting that gives a sense of the surreal and, in turn, the symbolic, and haunted by Conrad, too, with the probing of just how dark the human heart must sometimes be to act on such absurd irrationality that has dictated too much of history. Because Coetzee is South African and because the details of the novel (the uniforms, the horses, the soldiers, etc.) seem of the nineteenth century, it would be easy to view this as only a story from his own troubled land's past. But again, there is something much larger about the material here, and it also has echoes of the American West, where the Native Americans were seen as "barbarians," or even, more recently, Vietnam, where a communist people were often considered the same. Much of the comment cuts to the bone in its universality. For instance, when the Magistrate is frustratedly heartbroken at the sight of the battered prisoners, he tries to imagine the convoluted way the leaders of the Empire rationalize their assaults: "It would be best if this obscure chapter in the history of the world were terminated at once, if these people were obliterated from the face of the earth in order to make a new start, to run an empire in which there would be no more justice, no more pain."

The first-person narration is expertly paced, seething with suspense. In Coetzee's first book, *Dusklands,* which juxtaposed two interacting novellas, he demonstrated a striking ability to describe the physical, often in all of its bodily rankness, and that ability is equally evident here. And the scenes involving the Magistrate and the young barbarian woman work so well, each character emerging as a convincing jumble of strong and sometimes contradictory emotions. In short, this is a novel that does deserve the appellation tour de force, and I suppose that for me the sole problem, albeit a minor one, is the tendency to overdo and turn heavy-handed with the several passages concerning a symbolic dream of a child in the snow the Magistrate repeatedly has.

At end of Cavafy's poem "Waiting for the Barbarians," the people in an unnamed land don't know what is going to happen to them; the barbarians never showed up, and having the barbarians to fear and think about offered "a kind of solution," gave them something with which to occupy themselves. At the end of Coetzee's novel, the situation is somewhat similar. Is our lot as supposedly civilized human beings hopeless, and is Coetzee telling us that we need, and always have needed, somebody to persecute and hate? Or is the Magistrate, the figure Joll charges with attempting to egotistically make a name for himself as "the one just man," a valid hope? Can we, in fact, believe in the individual who, because he won't readily submit, won't easily be broken, even after much brutally inhuman treatment, possesses the power to prove that history isn't an unfeeling and frightening machine, and it doesn't have to repeat itself, after all—if somebody simply takes a stand to announce a saner way?

—Africa Today, 1983

A Bend in the River, by V. S. Naipaul

A few years ago, V. S. Naipaul published *Guerrillas*, a novel set in an imaginary Caribbean country. It didn't paint a very becoming picture of the contemporary political situation in that part of the Third World, to say the least. His latest novel, *A Bend in the River*, takes place in an imaginary African country, and it seems to use similar brush strokes to paint the same type of picture of this developing area.

The story is narrated in the first person by an East African of Indian descent, Salim. He leaves his cushy, but doomed, life in his troubled native land on the Indian Ocean to take over a general goods store in an alternatingly dusty and jungled African country, well inland. His narration builds in introspection and digression, as a lonely Salim slowly chronicles his several years in the city located at the bend in a river. The principals include: a cold, politicized son of a trading bush woman who sees himself as the New African; an old friend of Salim's family who sets up an African exchange-scholar program, which he knows from the start is a total sham; the handsome Belgian wife of a burnt-out white Africanist at the national university, a woman whose perfunctory lust has no chance of rescuing Salim from his growing malaise; and, ominously, the Big Man. Salim never meets the Big Man, but this dictator of the country, so named, haunts the lives of all the characters. His blown-up photograph in traditional garb is posted throughout the city, and youth squads are made to parade along the red-dirt streets, through the shantytowns and past the high garbage heaps, each marcher brandishing a booklet of the Big Man's quotations as if it were a powerful weapon.

The novel is essentially plotless, though anything as positive as a well-defined, structuring plot would be at odds with the underlying mood of pessimism—a feeling resulting from the country's pandemic listlessness, confusion, and even unmitigated evil. That isn't to say the novel lacks drive. Salim's voice alone becomes the real attraction. It is an intriguing running commentary built on precise detail and probing intelligence. For instance, plagued by guilt after an afternoon tryst with the Belgian woman Yvette, Salim thinks: "I had my first alarm about myself, the beginning of decay of the man I had known myself to be. I had visions of beggary and decrepitude; the man not of Africa lost in Africa, no longer with the strength of purpose to hold his own and with less claim to anything than the ragged, half-starved old drunks from the villages who wandered about the square, eyeing food stalls, cadging mouthfuls of beer, and the young troublemakers from the shantytowns, a new breed who wore shirts stamped with the Big Man's picture and talked about foreigners and profit and wanting only money . . ."

Writing of this mythical country, Naipaul repeatedly uses the general term "Africa" and he seems to be addressing himself to all of independent sub-Saharan black Africa. So, finding this book waiting for review upon returning from a stay in that Africa, as happened to me, is somewhat troubling. I must say that Naipaul takes on the task that many non-African novelists who have written well lately about the continent have usually avoided. He delivers serious realism, without using Africa for fantasy, as John Updike did in *The Coup,* or dark humor, as Paul Theroux has done in a couple of novels. I also have to admit that there is much to support his grim conclusions in today's Africa—frequent bloodshed in local wars and the high life of Mercedes and posh villas for corrupt government officials while the rest of the population can often find just feeding itself a perpetual harrowing struggle.

On the other hand, I like to think that Naipaul's assessment of independent Africa's present situation is accurately reflected in the title, *A Bend in the River*—a wrong turn, the worst that *could* happen in many new African countries and probably already has happened in a few, certainly the Central African Empire and Uganda. Truth of the matter is that I can't completely go along with this pessimism when I remember many scenes from my own travel, sometimes only an incident very minor, a single passing moment in the course of a day, but revealing the larger, nevertheless. Once while walking around in downtown Yaoundé, Cameroon, I took a small plastic bag of orange peelings and crumpled candy bar wrappers out of my shoulder bag and tossed it in a streetside litter basket, despite the fact the street itself was heaped with foul-smelling refuse. The men selling cheap shirts and flimsy suitcases spread out on the dusty sidewalk smilingly watched me, maybe perplexed at first but then shouting their approval, a bunch of them, with one offering the universal salute sign.

Naipaul has delivered an artistically deft and fully worthwhile book. Again, though, I personally would have appreciated some mention of that optimistic spirit, if only in a character who gets trampled in life, sad to say, for bravely espousing it. At least it would have been there. And, believe me, granting there are so many major problems and looming woes, it *is* there in Africa.

—*America Magazine*, 1979

July's People, by Nadine Gordimer
and Up Against Apartheid, by Richard Pollak

In one of her earlier novels, *The Conservationist*, Nadine Gordimer told the story of a rich white South African businessman. The book's essentially realistic portrayal often shifted to an almost surrealistic plane. Gordimer seemed to be saying that life in contemporary South Africa was often such a lunatic affair—for whites as well as nonwhites—that it could take on the texture of an ominous dream.

July's People, Gordimer's latest novel, is set in a near future, at a time when South Africa has exploded in civil strife. Black revolutionaries strike from bases permitted them by the black government in neighboring Mozambique. They battle the forces of a weakening white government in the big cities, while the white civilians flee abroad. In the midst of this, a white family, the Smales, abandon their once-comfortable home in the Johannesburg suburbs to hide in the village of their long-time black servant, July, far out in the veldt.

One one hand, Gordimer is creating a situation that is hypothetical and futuristic. However, she also may again be probing that dreamlike plane. For many whites in South Africa today, the looming disaster of a successful black revolt must be a constant concern, the kind of thought that presses on the brain, what one surely dreams about, nightmarishly.

Bam Smales and his wife Maureen are liberals. He is an architect and she a former ballet student, both with records of deep social concern for blacks and condescending distaste for many of their racist Afrikaner compatriots. They escape the tide of battle with their three children in a yellow *bakkie,* a rugged sport utility truck. From the beginning they are uneasy as July's guests. He is a polite and unusually quiet man, who used to be given Wednesdays and alternate Sundays off and would return then to his village (actually just a cluster of huts) to visit his wife and own children every two years.

Events are seen from the alternating points of view of the different characters, though most of the story is devoted to Maureen. She waits and watches: as her children learn to eat with their fingers and soon are part of the shabbiness of the village scene; as her husband has to back down and lose face in arguments with local men over the use, and even the ownership, of his truck and hunting rifle; and as a portable radio, their sole contact with the outside world and their former life (repeatedly referred to as "back there"), tells of only more rocket attacks and confused fighting.

This is a stunning, very moving novel. Gordimer's observation is poetically exact, especially in chronicling the hard and seamy life of the rural blacks that assaults Maureen's senses. The uneasy apprehension over what will become of Maureen and her family soon gives way to a more compelling suspense: What will come next in their crash-course in deep self-discovery (she has already figured she is not what she thought she was, an understanding, compassionate liberal) now that survival is at stake? The dialogue has all the intensity of searing stage drama, and the strongest exchanges pit her against July. She at last realizes that July is a man with needs and aspirations of his own, somebody with as little understanding of her as she has of him.

But her family's lives depend utterly on him; eventually he will let her know it.

■

Richard Pollak's *Up Against Apartheid* offers a fresh study of the media in race-mad South Africa. Pollak, the literary editor of *The Nation*, provides a grim account of government censorship under apartheid. Journalists supposedly are allowed a good deal of freedom, but for a conscientious reporter the country's mine field of strict press laws can lead to imprisonment and even torture. It is not a question of an outright totalitarian control; it is the trickier situation of the reporter constantly not knowing where he or she stands vis-a-vis the byzantinely repressive statute books. Pollak reports in detail on the so-called Muldergate scandal (named after a past minister of information, Cornelius P. Mulder), which involved a massive government propaganda effort. One of the improprieties was the secret transfer of substantial government money in a far-fetched attempt to buy the *Washington Star* daily newspaper in 1975 and use it as an international propaganda outlet. Pollak also argues particularly well the need for the English-language press in South Africa as opposed to the Afrikaans, claiming that it remains truth's last hope in the country as currently governed.

Much of the book echoes Gordimer's sense of the dreamlike—how again and again apartheid has given South Africa a life that must not seem real whatsoever. Case in point: In an introductory discussion of the general situation in this country where nonwhites outnumber whites by approximately five to one, Pollak quotes from a report on token integration found in the *Survey of Race Relations in South Africa*, an annual compendium and assessment of actual racial policies, focusing on Johannesburg: "Only black visitors bearing foreign passports could use all hotel facilities. Other blacks could not drink in men's-only bars. . . . They could swim if resident at the hotel, and be served liquor at mixed-sex bars if resident or bona fide guest of a resident. Blacks who were not resident could be served liquor only if they were taking or about to take a meal on the premises, or attending a function, such as a conference."

You know, it would be laughable, if it weren't so, yes, truly nightmarish.

—*The Progressive*, 1982

African Airports: A Poem

Long after returning
You dream of them incessantly.
It seems you are always en route,
Always late and waiting
To lift off again,
Inside the cramped DC's cabin or slouched
In a waiting room chair, sculpted fiberglass.
In Lagos' futuristic concrete monstrosity,
You wander through
The deserted Transit Passenger gift shops;
In the bar of Lome's little facility,
You sit amid sunglassed blacks
(their sport shirts pink from the dust)
Imbibing tall bottles of local beer.
In Cameroon in the rainy season—
The jungle beyond the airstrip's velvet
So gray—the banker from Morgan
Sitting beside you on the plane says he read
Of golden lions yesterday attacking
Three baggage handlers at dawn;
Only one is expected to live.
Mechanical problems,
And the dark-uniformed stewardesses are
Again telling you to get off

In the night; you learn to distinguish the styles
Of berets the military men wear.
You try to overhear
Some ragged Congolese women chatting in French.
And back home,
In the outskirts of Boston or hushed New York,
You awake in the blue moonlight,
Careful not to disturb your wife,
And go to the kitchen, where around
The yellow appliances you know
You will find all the tired travelers,
Talking of exchange rates and delays,
The wonderful ways of the weary.

—*William and Mary Review*, 1982

June 2

A Brief, Very Personal History of Portuguese Literature

1. Pensão Brasil-África

I've been in Lisbon for a few days.

And now I am stretched out on the bed, still dressed and reading from Fernando Pessoa's *The Book of Disquiet,* nine at night.

Then maybe I just place the book beside me on the made bed. I doze off, to awake an hour or so later, having slipped into an easy dream, soon dissolving.

Alone, I am staying in the Pensão Brasil-África.

■

A modest but quite homey place on a short side street, the Brasil-África occupies the top floor of an old apartment building. It has an ornate blue-and-white tile facade and iron-railed balconies rife with well-watered geraniums. I like how the location is central, a few blocks away from the entirely regal esplanade of the Praça do Comércio, which opens up to a fine panorama of the wide River Tagus. Waking, it takes me a little time to get oriented, realize exactly where I am. I suppose I know that one of the small pleasures of travel is to wake in a room in an unfamiliar place, almost still in the dream you were having (was it something about Marion—or I'll call her that here—a woman from Baton Rouge whom I sometimes wonder if maybe I should have married when young; we'd met as students at a writers' conference to which I'd received a scholarship; I remember we joked, laughingly back then, agreeing that with so much romance rampant among attendees, most any summer writers' conference, such as ours in the rolling green hills of Vermont, probably had more to do with just that—romance, all but scenarios from the old TV show *The Love Boat*—than what normally constitutes writing-workshop instruction), yes, there is a feeling half jarring but half soothing as well, to coming out of sleep that way with a sense of disorientation, even a soft lostness, looking around, asking yourself where in the world you are . . . until you do, in fact, recognize enough of the surroundings to return once more to what commonly passes for the here and now.

I slowly pivot and sit up on the bed's edge in the spacious, high-ceilinged room.

■

I look around some more. There's a single lamp on the night table, glowing, a glossy orange porcelain base and conical parchment shade; there are the bedspread's bright pastel stripes, the cracked yellow walls and the brown linoleum floor, the heavy Portuguese furniture, such dark wood for the huge armoire and the vanity/desk with its clouded mirror, a couple of intricately carved, straight-backed chairs to match. There are the long gauzy curtains on either side of the open French doors that give way to a balcony here on the top floor, the fourth, as reached by winding wooden stairs, creaky.

And fully awake now, I do know for certain where I, well, *am*.

I'm wearing old khakis and a long-sleeve dress shirt with the sleeves rolled up, the collar open, comfortable travel attire. Sweating a bit in the warmth, I think of Marion from Baton Rouge some more, wondering why she chose this time and place to turn up in a dream when I hadn't thought of her for so long. I stare at the paperback that I'd let drop beside me when I dozed off, a copy of Fernando Pessoa's *The Book of Disquiet*; it's more or less the reason why I am here in Lisbon for these two weeks, rereading and thinking about the work of Pessoa, others in Portuguese literature, too. I've been doing a lot of this kind of travel lately, going to a place where literature I love is set, immersing myself in the world of the words of the other country for a while. And this time it is, very much so, Pessoa, the great modernist poet of twentieth-century Portuguese literature. He died in 1935 at age forty-seven, a decidedly lonely bachelor working as a clerk in a Lisbon office and relatively unknown then, probably most admired today for his posthumously published meditations of a fictional Lisbon office worker, Bernardo Soares, somebody quite like Pessoa, of course. I am staring at the cover of the Penguin Classics edition of the book. It has a dark design, with the top half a black-and-white photo that shows a man, his face not visible, in a baggy suit, standing with arms wildly raised in a sudden gesture of either absolute exasperation or absolute ecstasy before a planked doorway in what seems to be a cramped alley in Lisbon, a white mosaic sidewalk below of the sort that are ubiquitous in the hilly city; in front of him, a well-groomed younger man in neat slacks and what looks like a golf cardigan, his hair a 1950s pomp, recoils in amazement at the gesture, taken aback in an utter blinded-by-the-light posture, obviously surprised to see the behavior of this older man he has just come upon in such a wild state. The cover's only true color, a bright orange, appears on the publisher's colophon of the pudgy penguin in the middle of a horizontal white band dividing the photograph on top from the lower half, very black, where it says, with the author's name large and in that orange again, then the rest in white on the black:

Fernando Pessoa

The Book of Disquiet

Edited and Translated by Richard Zenith

I pick up the book there beside me from the bedspread, turn it over to look again at the photo credit on the back, which notes: "Cover Photograph: Lisbon 1957, by Gérard Castello-Lopes." The cover is perfect, I tell myself, aptly capturing the often startling tenor of Pessoa's hefty volume, a book assembled from pages of sometimes random jottings found in a large wooden trunk in his meager lodgings at the time of his death (I've already seen a hokey full-size model of that famous trunk—freshly varnished wooden planks, the box filled with concocted crumpled typewritten pages—at the city's Casa Fernando Pessoa, a cultural center on Rua Coelho da Rocha, where they have set up a facsimile of his bedroom complete with mandatory trunk; I found the place somewhat disappointing when I visited the day before, not enough about Pessoa and it seeming more of an art gallery and gift shop than anything else)—in fact, the cover is beyond perfect, I decide. It echoes the haunting, indefinable metaphysical essence of the posthumously published book, page after pulpy paperback page of diary-style entries numbered in dark bold by the assembling editor.

I open the book to where a little pocket-notebook sheet serves as a place marker, and I realize that I'd fallen asleep in the midst of doing what I have been doing every night while in Lisbon; strange, but it seems the best way to read Pessoa's masterpiece now that I am here.

■

Actually, having been in Lisbon for these few days, I do the same thing every night.

I've read *The Book of Disquiet* before, two or three times, and having brought this copy to Lisbon, I've discovered a fresh, seemingly revealing method to approach it on this trip, for me one better suited than a normal chronological reading. In truth, *The Book of Disquiet* with its many numbered entries—481 of them, plus a supplement containing yet more that are unnumbered—isn't a novel whatsoever, as it occasionally gets billed and, according to that label, supposedly the life story of that lonely and dreaming Lisbon office worker, Bernardo Soares; rather, it's more so an extended meditation on the troubling perplexity of life itself— some entries like philosophical prose poems on large subjects, such as unrequited love and the ultimate transiency of our existence, others more straightforward mini-narratives, as in one that expresses Soares's awkwardness when an office-staff group photograph is taken and upon seeing the result he's struck by his pathetic demeanor, an undeniable personal insignificance. But no matter what the topic, everything is always laced with an intense cutting honesty and a longing *to really know*.

So each evening in the Brasil-África I have stretched out on the bed and flipped through the pages as if fingering a deck of cards, to see where

I randomly land, which adds an appropriate additional measure of sheer chance to it all, considering that the book was simply put together from the often unsorted pages in that trunk; then I've opened up the volume to the spot where I stopped, to read and fully contemplate the entry, not that much different from studying a religious text, I guess. I have been doing this for exactly three entries each night. On a blank end page, inside the back cover, I've used a soft pencil to jot down the evening's date and also the numerals of the entries. Sometimes I've underlined in faint pencil specific lines in the passages themselves.

True, I must have dozed off right after reading my three for this night, so tired after my hours of walking throughout sunny Lisbon during the day. And I wonder now if possibly something within one of those entries seeped from the black print on the flimsy paperback pages, little more than newsprint, onto the big screen of the otherworld of what I'd been dreaming.

About Marion, from Baton Rouge, very long ago.

Still sitting up on the bed's edge, book in hand, I find again the three entries for this evening, June 17, 2016, as marked in pencil in back— 63, 288, and 266. I read them, or, more exactly, look over what I have underlined in each:

■

63

The entire life of the human soul is mere motions in the shadows. We live in a twilight of consciousness, never in accord with whom we are or think we are. . . . Like someone on a hill who tries to make out the people in the valley, I look down on myself from on high, and I'm a hazy and confused landscape, along with everything else.

288

How tragic not to believe in human perfectibility!
And how tragic to believe in it!

When I first came to Lisbon I used to hear from the apartment above ours, the sound of scales played on a piano, the monotonous practicing of a girl I never actually saw. Today I realize that in the cellar of my soul, by some mysterious process of infiltration, those scales persist . . .

■

I place the book down on the made-up bed. I stand, stiff indeed from much walking that afternoon, somewhat sunburned, too, despite having loaded up with sunblock gunk.

Earlier, I'd been seeking out some spots associated with Pessoa's life, deep into the Bairro Alto district, now trendy with its clubs and bars. Nevertheless, in a cul-de-sac there remains, still completely operational, the French hospital where Pessoa (shy, a heavy drinker) died of liver failure; it's a quaint little white stucco operation with a small courtyard, quieter than quiet. Then, closer to the river, I stopped by the Café A Brasileira (Brazilian Lady Café), the foremost landmark in what today is virtually an ongoing national celebration of Pessoa, who lately has become almost the icon for all contemporary Portuguese culture itself. Art nouveau for its colorful facade, the Brasileira was the meeting place for literary types of Pessoa's day, and now it offers a bronze statue of a seated Pessoa—bespectacled and with a thin, brushy mustache, wearing a business suit and a 1930s fedora—amid terrace umbrella tables in front, tourists actually lining up to take turns having themselves photographed sitting next to the figure in an empty adjoining bronze chair provided. I'd ducked my head into the Brasileira before, just to see the fine interior with its black-and-white tile floors, oil paintings on the high, rose-colored walls, and no shortage of gleaming brass and fine mahogany throughout, but never ordered anything, not even a beer or a simple coffee; the whole scene looked too touristy, as this afternoon I again decided to continue walking. I kept going, clear up to the old Moorish castle that sits on the highest hill above the city, exploring the sometimes ramshackle surrounding neighborhoods for a couple of hours, definitely too much tramping around altogether for one day. No wonder I dozed off while reading after a good dinner at a cubbyhole place I just happened to spot in the ancient Alfama district, a working-class bar not much bigger than a good walk-in closet and only a chalkboard out front, no menus inside. With the little Portuguese I have, I conversed when ordering with the comically gruff waiter/proprietor about the grilled fish of the day—*linguado;* flounder—which turned out to be delicious. In the Brasil-África now I go over to the room's small oval sink (the bathroom proper is down the hall) and splash some cool water on my face, which feels good. I pat it dry with the nicely stiff white towel smelling of bleach, then walk across that lumpy brown linoleum (the Brasil-África is pretty basic, thirty euros a night) to the balcony, pushing the long organdy curtains aside.

Out on the balcony the air is warm and humid, summery, and I can hear a burst of cheering in the distance for the Euro Cup soccer match broadcast on a massive Jumbotron that Carlsberg Beer has set up there at the Praça do Comércio, crowds assembling in that huge square every evening right beside the Tagus; somebody must have just scored, but who is playing and in what stadium it is in up in France, the host country for the competition, I have no idea—not Portugal tonight, I know, or the noise, accompanied by a cacophony of blaring car horns after any good play, would be loud all over the city. I was there myself the evening before, bought a beer in a plastic cup at one of the Carlsberg counters and stood with the crowd and watched.

I look at the near-full moon now, slightly lopsided above the tile rooftops and moving in and out of shredded, ivory-colored clouds.

I stand out on the balcony for a while, hands on the cool black iron railing, thinking about Pessoa, then thinking about the trip I plan to take in a day or so, to spend the night in the Medieval university town of Coimbra, high in the central mountains—I've heard a good deal about the region's rare beauty, so I'm really looking forward to that. And I'm also thinking some more about Marion, it seems. There was something about a Boy Scout shirt, I tell myself, perhaps the sole shard of the dream remaining.

And who knows how long I stand out there in the night.

■

... *because it seems there were evenings in Vermont, there at Bread Loaf summer conference where we were both students, 1973, no 1974, and Marion had this way of wearing a simple Boy Scout shirt, khaki and with embroidered patches, troop number in white on red and such, probably a thrift store thing, she would wear it like a light jacket with a top and her shorts on those cool nights in Vermont, the sleeves neatly folded back to the elbow, she was willowy, bobbed auburn hair and a snub nose, big eyes, she was lovely enough to have actually once been in an Italian director's movie filmed in Baton Rouge when a teenager, she was freelancing articles now and teaching in a poetry-in-the-schools program in Baton Rouge, and I might be late to getting to wherever we were going to, yes, rendezvous, our having met only days before but somehow enamored with each other immediately, and I was pretty untethered in life then, having canned daily newspaper work, the grind of police reporting and, worse, soporific city hall reporting, I was trying to write short stories and a first novel, and having been given what was a work scholarship to be a waiter at the conference, wearing a white tunic on the job, clowning around as I served everybody else in my fiction workshop class at dinner, I maybe took pride in the fact that I wasn't paying for the two weeks of residency, the endless readings, the endless talk about books, all of it heady fare, fun, the scholarship was based on manuscript submission, seemingly some validation of the worth of my yet to be published fiction, if nothing else, and after banging around in the kitchen as things got cleaned up I would meet up with her every evening, she was thirty, a few years older than me, I often later wondered if my hesitation after that summer in following through with getting together again once we left Vermont, continuing the relationship as something more than a summer affair, she back in Baton Rouge, me back in seaside Rhode Island, there was letter writing, I wondered if it was due to our ages and how three years and anybody being thirty could seem such a large gap to me at twenty-seven, my very foolishly thinking that mattered, and it meant nothing, of course, and it might be at an evening reading by a* big-name writer where she would save a seat for me, or once I was late in meeting her at a dance they were holding in the cavernous assembly room, formerly a genuine livestock barn, and she was waiting for me there in that Boy Scout shirt, almost chic like that, the sleeves folded back neatly to the elbow as usual, yes, the shirt unbuttoned and tails loose as if a light jacket, there was thumping Rolling Stones music at the dance, and she had such an alluring, gentle Louisiana drawl, very exotic to me, whispery as she smiled, and she also had, the way I remember it, the deep sadness of a very brief marriage to a college boyfriend and their living and working for a year in New York City, though that hadn't worked out, she told me the whole story, how painful a divorce could be, even embarrassing when so young, she was admirably honest about everything there in Vermont, vulnerable, her poetry was quite wonderful, and because . . . and . . . because . . .

■

Still out on the balcony, I push my hand through my hair.

I walk back into the room, knowing that, man, I'm tired and then some, after those hours of walking and walking that day. Stretched out on the bed again, back propped against the headboard, I work the little fifty-buck Wal-Mart tablet with a keyboard I use for travel, taking care of some email replies back home and booking online a hotel in Coimbra, where I know I will be in a couple of days.

2. Talking Under the Eye (Singular) of Camões

"The translation they did of my book was good," Jacinto says.

"You're lucky," I say.

"It was a nice-looking book, too," he goes on. "They paid me right on time. I went to New York to give a reading, and part of the America trip was also visiting a couple of colleges, one a state college in Massachusetts near Cape Cod."

"U. Mass Dartmouth," I say. "Not to be confused with Dartmouth

College, but that's the town—near Cape Cod, like you say—where it is, Dartmouth. A lot of Portuguese live in New Bedford and on the Cape, they originally were known as expert fishermen. I grew up in Rhode Island, close by. U. Mass Dartmouth does quite a bit in Portuguese literature, no?"

"Yes. And the trip went really well. When I read my work in the States, I got more laughs than I've ever gotten. That was good, the laughs."

He smiles widely.

"You're could be right about that," I say, "and it's always best not to read serious stuff at a public reading. Not that I'm a big fan of giving readings myself, content to let the work hopefully survive as it should, on the page, but when I've done them I try to avoid anything very serious."

■

I am sitting outdoors at a wobbly metal table with the Portuguese novelist Jacinto Lucas Pires, a slightly built, forty-something guy, bearded, in a T-shirt, jeans, and a newsboy cap. It seems that a recent book of my own was brought out by the same publisher that did an English translation of one of Jacinto's novels, *The True Actor* (a wild story of an unemployed actor who gets involved with a certain Lisbon call girl favored by the Portuguese rich), and through the mutual publisher—a smaller independent but honorable operation—I was put in contact with him, along with the suggestion that we should definitely meet when I was in Lisbon. And now at noontime at the email-arranged spot and time, we are talking.

We take advantage of the leafy shade of the trees at one end of the Praça de Camões, a city square (*praça* in Portuguese) that is actually a park-like oval. We are having coffee while the heavy auto traffic rotates about the park; old yellow Lisbon trolleys grind by now and then as well, the overhead connections sparking bright. In the center of the tiled Praça de Camões, atop an ornate pedestal, rises an imposing bronze statue of the most important writer in the entire history of Portuguese literature, the country's combined Homer and Dante and Shakespeare, if you will—Luís Vaz de Camões, author of what is indisputably a national epic, *The Lusiads* (*Os Lusíadas*).

In thoroughly rhapsodic language, Camões's poem tells a mythical version of explorer Vasco da Gama's discovery of an ocean route to India, complete with a cast of hovering gods and a threatening sea monster. It's a patriotic paean to the amazing age of fifteenth/sixteenth-century Portuguese exploration, when due to innovation in navigational study (think Prince Henry the Navigator himself) and state-of-the-art design for their deft, three-masted caravels, the Portuguese gradually extended the empire of this small mountainous kingdom first to Goa in India and then around the Cape of Good Hope to Macau in China, during that period also venturing clear across the Atlantic to Brazil and claiming an immense chunk of South America for the crown. A swashbuckling, always rebellious figure, Camões (1524–1580) led a privileged life until his pursuit of a beautiful courtier resulted in exile by the king; he soldiered in Morocco, losing an eye in battle with the Moors, then set off to sea. His apparent early misfortune became a most fortunate break, in a way, because this checkered wandering stint of about twenty years as a sailor—including a shipwreck off Cambodia, where he nearly drowned, and even facing trial by his own government in Goa for some shady monetary dealings—provided firsthand experience indeed for a maritime epic. The pigeon-splattered bronze likeness of him might be straining for effect in portraying the rugged adventurer overromantically, here with a long flowing cape and lowered knight's saber, a laurel wreath atop his curly locks, but one can't deny the monument's essential *stature,* at least two stories high: passing by it a few times prior to this day, I've been repeatedly struck by the metaphorical appropriateness of that very size.

My iced coffee in a clear glass has lemon and cinnamon in it, no cream, the way the Portuguese do drink iced coffee, Jacinto explained to me when we first ordered at the little blue kiosk in this corner of the park, to take our drinks to the wrought iron table and chairs under the shading trees. Jacinto keeps smiling as he talks, sometimes a scratch at his spade-shaped beard or a quick tug at the visor of that newsboy cap.

I ask him how a writer of hopefully serious fiction gets by in Portugal without the opportunity for teaching work, as I know creative writing courses are seldom if ever offered in universities here. He says there's hustling necessary to get by, but a quite satisfying hustling, nevertheless. He talks about a soccer column he writes for a newspaper, also a serial he is writing for a children's radio show, adding that while there is an occasional opportunity to do something at a Portuguese university, a lecture with a short workshop, perhaps, it usually is pretty much a break-even proposition at best, when one considers time lost and often travel expenses; further, he isn't convinced writing can be taught, anyway. I have to admit to him that after a long time on campuses teaching creative writing myself, I, too, wonder if it can be taught, and I explain that when younger I was a daily-newspaper reporter writing my own fiction in every spare moment outside of work I could find, producing a decent amount then maybe because it did entail stolen, and therefore always treasured, time. Still, I try to defend the teaching of creative writing as a humanizing exercise, if nothing else, helping students to read better by seeing literature from the inside in their attempting to write some of it themselves; however, I confess that the unavoidable downside of a campus job is being surrounded by the safe, middlebrow outlook that universities can thrive on and the administrative pettiness that surely is inherent to any bureaucratic operation, which can gnaw at you over time. I tell him I usually have little or nothing in common, if honest, with so-called scholarly colleagues, whose work in an English department nowadays, if I'm *really* honest, often appears to have little or nothing to do with the magic of words and literature's power, as sincere as they are about it, the approach to the study of literature currently stressing the topical, more akin to formulaic sociology or political science than anything else.

He smiles.

I ask him more questions about Portuguese literature. I explain, or try to, how I take trips like this one, my time in Portugal, to immerse myself in the work of the writer I greatly admire from another country, seeing if anything different happens by reading that work in the place where it's set. And he goes on to talk about Pessoa. I tell him how an Irish novelist once said to me that any writer not from Ireland will never understand what it's like living under the shadow of Joyce, and I ask him if it might be a similar situation with Pessoa for a Portuguese novelist. But with a sigh he simply says Pessoa is *Pessoa*, there is no envy or shadow, only pure pride and continual admiration, adding that there was, of course, such a sadness to the man's life, living alone as he did, never marrying, no children (Jacinto has told me he has four, one reason he must generate a steady income, I figure, even if his wife does have a good professional job). And then I ask him about the two major contemporary Portuguese novelists, both of whose work I read a good deal of before setting out on the trip, José Saramago and António Lobo Antunes.

Saramago's fiction is metaphysical, usually with imaginative, fable-like premises for his novels, such as the idea of the Iberian Peninsula floating away from the European continent in *The Stone Raft*. Lobo Antunes's work is also dreamlike, but in a different way, frequently more than mere surrealism and close to outright hallucinatory. This atmosphere begins to emerge in his early book, *South of Nowhere*, based on his time serving as a young drafted medical doctor in the smoldering wasteland of Angola during his country's drawn-out unpopular war there that established Angola's independence from Portugal, a conflict similar to our painful Vietnam experience (and the title I just gave is the novel's comparatively tame English-translation version; the original translates literally as *The Assholes of Judas*), and then it gets vented fully, that nightmarish quality, in later novels such as *What Can I Do When Everything's on Fire*, dealing with the contemporary Lisbon nightclub underworld of drugs and sexual obsession. It seems there had been competition between the two novelists while Saramago was alive (he died in 2010), and I tell Jacinto how I once read that when Saramago won the Nobel Prize in Literature in 1998, the first from his nation to do so, a reporter from a major Lisbon newspaper, possibly the prestigious *Diário de Notícias*, called Lobo Antunes up asking if he had a comment, to which Lobo Antunes only curtly—and aptly, when you consider the intraprofessional rivalry—replied, "I think you have the wrong number," then promptly hung up.

"That is very funny, I hadn't heard it before," Jacinto says.

"It could just be a story," I say, as Jacinto notes that many people in Portugal remain divided on their favorite, will still argue about it.

"Maybe like a Stones versus the Beatles sort of thing, way back in my day," I add. "You had to champion one or the other."

"Yes, yes."

■

We talk about Saul Bellow, whose work Jacinto loves. We talk about the differences between French and Portuguese novels. Jacinto says that as much as he admires French work, it lately seems to have been reduced to but an intellectual game, which is largely true, and we talk about how—and surprising to me as somebody who has published my share of short story collections—the situation for the acceptance of that genre is even worse in Portugal than in the U.S. I know that Jacinto has won a number of awards for his work, is considered a prominent Portuguese writer, but he says that he published a book of his own short stories the previous year without a single review—or nothing until one that came out in a Lisbon newspaper six months later, when nobody seemed to care. We talk of Brazil, where I spent time when I was lucky enough to get invited to give some lectures (rather impromptu, I must admit, talks on Faulkner, Hemingway, and Fitzgerald) at a university in São Paulo. Jacinto has visited Brazil for the well-known international book festival in Paraty, an idyllic seaside resort town of retro hippies and plenty of beaches with sunshine and rattling palm trees; if a writer is prominent and *truly* lucky enough to get that invitation (forget those run-of-the-mill lectures I gave in urban São Paulo), it's an undeniable plum. We talk more of Pessoa and Lobo Antunes and Saramago, also Bellow.

And soon we are talking about our own writing, what fiction we are working on at the moment, and Jacinto begins telling me of a short story he has underway:

"You see, it's about a blind man who dreams up Borges's bedroom."

He gives more details of the story, and I almost forget where I am, finding myself caught up in the wonderful premise of the narrative itself, my calculating how it might work while he describes it, smiling some more.

"Man, I like it," I say. "I mean, I really like it. And could anything be more *Borgesian?*"

■

The yellow trolleys continue to grind by. More people have gathered on the surrounding stone benches, some unwrapping lunch packets; the brilliant June day is genuinely hot now, but I don't notice.

There's some talk about politics and the creeping return of nationalism bordering on full-fledged fascism across Europe, along with our both laughing about the absurdity of a current U.S. presidential candidate like the crazy-haired, orange-mugged Donald J. Trump—I assure Jacinto that such a windy buffoon will *never* have a chance of actually being elected to anything in America. When I approach what I know is the touchy subject of Portugal's fascistic past, I realize I probably shouldn't go in that direction while in Portugal, such questioning of the country's historical mistakes and here with a person I've only just met; it could be as awkward as somebody approaching me as an American with the moral ugliness of segregated buses and bona fide hooded Klansman as recent as my own lifetime in the Jim Crow era of the American South. But I do ask him about the longtime dictatorship of António de Oliveira Salazar, the academic economist—blank-faced and well-groomed, always photographed in a neat business suit—who ruled his country as a police state for over thirty-five years, until 1968. In fact, in some of my own daily walking so far I did come across, on a side street, the former headquarters of his feared secret police, which operated under the acronym PIDE (Polícia Internacional e de Defesa do Estado); the substantial edifice—now pristinely sandblasted and divided up into, ironically, luxury condos—bears a plaque out front giving some brief and frank history of what was infamously known during the dictator's regime as "The Torture House." But Jacinto doesn't dodge the question. He explains that it had much to do with Catholicism back then, the rigid conservatism, chiefly and blindly religious, not unlike that in neighboring Spain under its dictator Franco. He thinks that Salazar himself was beyond Pessoa in his bleak bachelorhood, and I have read that even as head of state, Salazar, who had studied for the priesthood when young, was always somewhat of a boy, no indecorous love affairs, a chaste son devoted to the memory of his deceased, staunchly Catholic mother much of his adult life. "A very, very sad man," Jacinto says.

After a full two hours, we finally part, returning our glasses to the little stand for coffee and soft drinks; we shake hands and assure each other we must keep in touch.

As we go our separate ways, I stop to look back across the park's oval. I like how the tile patterning around the statue is arranged almost as if the spreading points of an oversize compass, suitable for honoring world-wandering Camões. I also like how in my gazing up at the statue in the sunshine now, the sky's clear, hard blue as a backdrop, Camões is certainly most suitably imposing. It may be true that the statue is way too romantic (Saramago himself once called it a near comical D'Artagnan pose with the dramatic flowing cape and long, lowered sword, right out of *The Three Musketeers*, he decides), but there's no denying, I assure myself, that the reproduction got the "eye" right. And an *eye* it is, singular, because one-eyed Camões, maimed in battle when young, is always depicted with the right hooded lid closed, nothing short of a trademark, as something now hits me:

From his vantage point, and the direction he is facing, Camões seems to be looking down to the Café A Brasileira just a block away, its sidewalk terrace of many white mushroom umbrellas and in the center there that other sculpture, a seated Pessoa with legs casually crossed.

Two very great writers on this sunny day maybe having some much larger, obviously more important communication themselves, across the centuries, though my talk about books with Jacinto was satisfying enough for me. I think how fine it is to back into such surprisingly good literary conversation now and then, especially when two people from places very far apart—though both crazy about writing, having that in common—do somehow get together as we have done. I mean, isn't the importance of books and literature in life sometimes absolutely amazing that way?

∎

I head directly back to the Pensão Brasil-África, weaving through the streets and alleyways, to scribble notes in the little shirt-pocket-size composition books I carry a supply of when traveling (marbleized covers like real composition books, four for a buck at the local dollar store in Austin, Texas, where I live and teach at the university, filling up a small stack of them to use for an essay like the one you are reading now); I know I want to get down as much of our talk as possible, while still fresh in my mind.

3. An Imaginary Sentence in an Imaginary Book Review

This particular evening, I am finishing up my meal at the aforementioned cubbyhole place in the Alfama, by now my regular spot in Lisbon for dinner; the fish specialty, always tastefully grilled, changes every day, though I know it could be some of the freshest, very best seafood I've ever enjoyed.

And I find myself doing it again, writing the opening line in my mind of an imaginary book review. Or perhaps only whimsically attempting to do that, even here in Lisbon as the trip is winding down. (The two weeks in Portugal have happened so quickly, the sort of phantom time outside of routine time that travel can be, paradoxical in that one's awareness is intense but also airy, granting there are the acutely lonely moments that are often a part of any solo travel—in truth, it's almost as if the two weeks, very packed, *didn't* happen: all the walking to track down literary landmarks; then the trip for a couple of days by sleek, speeding train northward through the green summer countryside to the stunning little city of Coimbra and its ascending clusters of houses tacked onto the side of a mountain topped by the Medieval university, where students still wear black academic gowns to classes over their T-shirts, jeans, and sneakers; then smaller moments, such as the fun, once I got back to Lisbon, in returning to the Pensão Brasil-África and having to buzz at the big maroon doors on the tiny cobbled street to enter the courtyard again: one of the two cheery middle-aged Portuguese ladies in their cleaning smocks who run the place, Plácida, sounded entirely pleased to hear it was me when I announced myself through the intercom's crackly static, "Senhor Peter," I said, and as always she also seemed proud to show her English, very basic, by responding emphatically, "Sim, *Mister* Peter). Yes, I am finishing up at that restaurant in the Alfama and telling myself that it now occurs to me how the ultimate commentary on Portuguese literature might, in fact, be a novel, Saramago's *The Year of the Death of Ricardo Reis,* an observation that could be worked into such an opening line of my imaginary review.

The Alfama is the old Moorish district of the city. Admittedly, the neighborhood can become unpleasantly thick with tourists, it being the epicenter for rather tacky clubs for the moaningly sorrowful *fado* music that tourists do flock en masse to hear. However, the little winding back-streets and alleys of clustered stucco houses, kids playing outside and wash hanging out on drooping lines everywhere, are authentic. It's the only sector of the city that was spared from the devastating Great Earthquake of All Saints' Day 1755; the upheaval rumblingly leveled nearly everything else, a powerful tsunami topping off the devastation. Lisbon's current center-city grid—geometrical, wholly elegant, with buildings in the Pombaline architectural manner that mixes baroque and neoclassical, definitely best seen in the handsome Praça do Comércio—was the result of a complete redesign and reconstruction after the tragedy. The tiny bar is stark and seems to have no name, it's that small, with only an occasional local from the neighborhood ambling in for a quick glass of wine at its stubby zinc counter, and as the sole customer for dinner in the place at seven or so (the majority of business is probably at lunch), I linger the way I have been lingering here on other evenings while in Lisbon. I sip the good coffee, flip through the tabloid daily newspaper left there on the table, the contents mostly soccer news and an impressively comprehensive amount of ads for various sexual services, many with thumbnail color photos. I'm thinking how I will miss Portugal, the kind of mood that inevitably sets in when any good trip finishes up, and also thinking more about Saramago's *The Year of the Death of Ricardo Reis*, still caught up in an imaginary book review, composing again an opening sentence or two in my mind. People walk by on the street outside; some glance within as they pass, my facing the open door while sitting here at the table (the place has just three small tables along the wall, in a row parallel to the counter); the proprietor is cleaning things up, preparing to close for the evening.

I used to write dozens of book reviews for newspapers and magazines when young, as I suspect many young unpublished or scantly published fiction writers do. I freelanced pieces to a variety of places, any outlet from the Catholic biweekly *Commonweal* to the then staunchly left-wing *New Republic* to the short-lived attempt at a weekend-newspaper edition of the *Wall Street Journal* called the *National Observer*. I even was part of a stable of regular reviewers for the now long-gone—and for many literary types revered—*Chicago Daily News* when I lived in Chicago for a while back then. There was something so right about going into the newsroom once a week, to proceed past the spread of desks and rattling typewriters to the back corner. There, the book review editor sat all but forgotten, hidden about as far away as possible from what was regarded by most people (though not the reviewers) as the "real news." Other young reviewers from that stable of us might be there, just hanging out; the editor—a middle-aged guy in rumpled shirtsleeves and loosened tie, an old hand at the rough Chicago newspaper trade—would open up the doors of a tall gray metal cabinet and lift out several review copies or bound galleys of the books he thought each of us might be interested in. In my case that sometimes meant volumes on Vietnam War protest and also what then in the 1970s was called the counterculture in general (occasionally covering that was the best of my beats when a daily-newspaper reporter around Boston right after college, so the editor automatically considered me an expert and it stuck in his mind), but more often, and if I was lucky, the assignments were good fiction. There was an excitement to receiving the books, just handling them in their glossy jackets and considering myself certainly a literary man of sorts as I started back to my small apartment with the stack. The editor would tell me to choose one or two that seemed worthwhile to write on, while he knew that I, as most of those young reviewers, would probably sell the rest to a used bookstore for needed pocket change: a life of freelance writing (I wrote some weekend-section feature articles, too, for the paper and its sister operation, the *Chicago Sun-Times*) with the odd hope of supporting oneself by that alone, was a deception that one could harbor only when extremely young and totally naive.

As time went by I reviewed less, and once I started publishing more of my own fiction and signed on for creative writing teaching jobs at colleges, responsibilities on those two fronts alone were increasingly enough to keep me occupied full-time; also, gradually disappearing was the essential need to see one's name in print on a review byline and therefore associated by dint of that with matters literary, additional slim evidence when starting out that I was perhaps involved and legitimately a *writer*.

But the habit of trying different opening sentences in my mind for an imaginary review of any book I read remains, an old exercise, lingering throughout life, it seems, and serving no other purpose than to see if I can get a bead on a book's essence. And now finishing up my meal, savoring the last sips from the demitasse of strong Portuguese coffee, I attempt to compose one—like this, let's say:

"For a good history of Portuguese literature as packed into the most intriguing novel so far by a modern master of that nation's literature, maybe of all world literature, then José Saramago's *The Year of the Death* of *Ricardo Reis*, in one sense, becomes exactly that in this strange, haunting tale of . . ."

But there are problems there, and the "strange, haunting tale" phrasing is weak, all right, also the sentence is already too long, straining to say too much before I zero in on needed description of the basic plot. And I know that attempting to reduce a novel to its thematic overlay is not the best way to start, more or less a dud when it comes to interesting anybody in a book you want to interest them in; nevertheless, "the most intriguing" tag would work, because it is surely Saramago's best book, for me, anyway. And the idea here would be to deliver a verdict directly, tip my hand right off as one sometimes does in a review when truly excited about the achievement, rather than rely on a standard old formula, the tried-and-true book review template that employs a calculated gradual approach of first giving a few paragraphs of calm summary, holding off on delivering any stauncher personal critical assessment till toward the very end.

At heart, *The Year of the Death of Ricardo Reis* is one great writer paying tribute to another, in this case Saramago showing his consummate respect for Pessoa and having as the book's protagonist one of Pessoa's own created literary personas. Pessoa wrote under many assumed names, which go well beyond simple pseudonyms, about seventy of them (he called them heteronyms), each identity quite different; among the better known are not only Bernardo Soares of *The Book of Disquiet* but also Ricardo Reis, a rather disillusioned physician and sometime poet whose classical odes, by Pessoa, are bravely stoical. According to the biographical note that Pessoa composed for him (Pessoa created life stories for many of the names he used), Reis emigrates from Portugal to Brazil, left there forever, it would seem, until Saramago's novel picks up with his life and shows him returning to Lisbon in 1936, shortly after the death of the actual Pessoa. Reis has a number of encounters with Pessoa as a ghost, all set against the backdrop of the rise of a brutal Salazar regime in Portugal and its iron-fisted Novo Estado (New State) right before World War II. But it's interesting how, in a wider sense, the book can come across as a tribute to the whole tradition of significant Portuguese literature. There are repeated references to Camões as well as occasional meditations and lovely asides concerning many of the country's important writers. At one point Saramago goes as far as including a revealing discussion that involves statues scattered throughout Lisbon that recognize such acknowledged luminaries, the list of them so honored providing an admirable line of descent: Camões, of course; then the Renaissance satirical playwright António Ribeiro, known as "O Chiado" (meaning "Squeak," and the central shopping district in the city bears his nickname); then the country's leading nineteenth-century novelist who wrote a series of thick naturalistic tomes, the Portuguese equivalent of Zola in that era, Eça de Queirós; and finally Pessoa himself, who is not yet memorialized by statuary in 1936 but emerges in the novel as spookily corporeal as any statue, with his presence woven throughout the novel as that recurring ghost (and what are statues, anyway, when you think of it, other than validly *corporeal* ghosts?).

I read *The Year of the Death of Ricardo Reis* before I set out on this trip. Though I haven't brought a copy of it with me to meditate on as I have done with Pessoa's book, I often go over to the famous, elegantly appointed Livraria Bertrand—it claims to be the oldest continually operating bookstore in the world, established in 1732—to read while standing some passages in a copy there (I simply can't buy any more books here, my small travel bag is overpacked already) and check again where various scenes are set in Lisbon.

And I have found myself wondering more about the novel. If this trip has been aimed at concentrating on Pessoa, Saramago's novel brilliantly does explore so much of the intent of Pessoa's own quest, with the character of a ghost, Pessoa, created by a writer, Saramago, and the ghost having successive meetings with a writer who was in turn created—very ghostily so—by Pessoa himself, Ricardo Reis.

Dizzying in its compounding effect, it's what might be seen in Nabokovian terminology as inducing that "metaphysical shiver," as Saramago's novel at times nearly *out-Pessoas* Pessoa.

■

And maybe I keep shifting around in my mind the imaginary review's opening sentence, until the proprietor in his green golf shirt and gray slacks (rugged at forty-five or so, short dark hair, a square jaw; he looks like he should be a black-jack dealer in Reno) returns from the steamy kitchen in back, where he has been chatting with whoever in his family does the cooking there, to ask me if everything was OK, the fish specialty this evening being dorade, flakily white and tastefully charred, garnished with thick tomato slices. He doesn't smile, yet appears satisfied that he has offered me, a traveler, a perfect dinner once more, the ten-euro *prix fixe* including a carafe of good red table wine plus always dessert and strong espresso; the dessert alone is well worth the visit, tonight a complicated meringue-topped puff pastry.

"*Muito bom,*" I say, knowing he also appreciates, man to man, that even such a basic phrase-book utterance, clunky, is my polite attempt not to reduce him to having to attempt to speak broken English, which, I have learned—as pathetically limited as my scant knowledge of Portuguese is—he absolutely refuses to do.

"*Muito bom,*" I repeat it.

Serious, he just nods, removes the remaining china from the paper-towel placemat, table size, then crumples up the placemat, a little clap of soft thunder in his strong hands. He goes back to the kitchen, and when he returns again, maneuvering sideways behind the short counter that is the bar, I step up to it, already with my pink ten-euro note in hand to pay, also a two-euro coin for a tip. Sure, I know that nobody is expected to tip in Portugal, it might even look hopelessly touristy in an everyday spot like this, tending toward insulting; yet, hell, this man deserves at least the small gesture of my appreciation, and there is a quality about his tough-guy, no-nonsense integrity that you have to admire. Or, it's especially refreshing for somebody like me after having been exposed to too much of the typical gushing American treatment back home—you know: "Hello, my name is April, I will be your server tonight and our specials are . . ." That type of tiresome mush.

Leaving the restaurant, I head up Alfama's steep incline, along rough-cobbled Rua dos Remédios and then along a couple more near-upright streets, narrow and zigzagging, toward the massive domed, strikingly white limestone church on a high hill there that now serves as the National Pantheon, an entombment site for several past presidents as well as (certifiably sacred to anybody Portuguese) Amália Rodrigues, the most celebrated of all *fado* singers; it's a landmark as prominent in the city's skyline on this eastern end as the Moorish castle is on Lisbon's very highest hill studding the exact center of the city. A wide plaza stretches before the stately Greek columns in front, and I sit down on the long steps leading up to this lofty perch. A teenage girl is looking after three boys about seven or eight who are kicking a soccer ball around that spreading plaza in front of the Pantheon's facade, and the noise doesn't bother me in the least; the kids' happy voices are musical, the occasional hollow echoing of the booted ball soothing in the evening's otherwise utter stillness, cooler up here.

I take out one of my little pocket notebooks, a half-dozen filled up on the trip already and this the last in my stock of them.

The cover is green marbleized (they alternate black, red, blue, and green, easy to keep track of that way), and sitting here in old khakis and another dress shirt with the sleeves rolled up, the collar open, I watch an attractive Portuguese couple, twenty-ish, stroll by on the winding street below, there at the foot of the long ascending steps; they are dressed in neat casual clothes, an arm of each over the other's shoulders and repeatedly veering off course and apparently laughing about the difficulty in such walking when linked together, obviously very happy, and I write down with the Bic how great it must be to be so *effortlessly young* like that. Then I write down, too, some details of the vista before me, looking out over the uneven clutter of the city's red-tile roofs below to the blue Tagus as wide as an inland sea, the little white ferries going this way and that to and from the small port town of Cacilhas across the way.

I suppose there is the rhythm of that soccer ball to listen to, the kids' excited voices, and I suppose I've forgotten about the imaginary book review, the sentence in my mind I never did finish, what I don't even make a note of. You can smell the sea up here, even discern, to the west and hazily softened by distance, where the river opens up to the enormous horizon of the Atlantic in earnest. It reminds me of how many ways Pessoa himself had to describe the sea in his writing, every description a little gem of a poem in itself.

■

It seems my imaginary sentence is surely now floating away somewhere out there.

■

The soccer ball, its black pentagons on white, scuffed, gets kicked awry, shot my way, and sitting on the steps I lean over to reach out and stop it with one hand before it bounces down them, then roll it back across the plaza to the kids. The kids in shorts and T-shirts look blankly at me, the pretty teenage girl taking care of them rolls her eyes, smiling, obviously apologetic for the boys having disturbed me. I offer a casual backwards wave with the Bic in hand, an indication of friendly dismissal, to assure her it's no problem whatsoever.

■

And the imaginary sentence, as maybe all sentences—imaginary or other-wise—eventually do, now floats farther and farther away out there, over that ocean so large and very aqua.

■

Eventually I start down the hill, walk the half-mile or so in the coming dark through the shadowy twisted streets and alleys of the Alfama to the Pensão Brasil-África. At the big maroon wooden doors there, arched, I press the intercom's button, speak into the little brass grill, and once more announce myself, saying:

"Senhor Peter."

There's the static, then I listen to cheery Plácida go through the routine yet again:

"Ah, *Mister* Peter," she says.

"Sim."

"Boa noite, *Mister* Peter."

My stay here has been pretty soothing, and how often does it take travel on one's own—with time to step back and re-evaluate things—to let one define for oneself who one really is and what is most important in life. For me it's frequently overindulgence in literature, which sometimes I suspect, as previously expressed elsewhere in my writing, that I've wasted far too much of my life on when I should have organized said life better on other fronts, probably not let relationships and a whole lot else fall apart along the way, perhaps even made an effort to marry somebody early on like lovely, soft-voiced Marion from the writers' conference in Vermont very long ago; and there have been dark moments recently when due the loss of two dear friends to terminal illnesses in rapid succession, then a serious medical issue of my own that came out of the proverbial nowhere (which fortunately did turn out OK), I have been confronted, discouragingly, with the oldest and largest question of all concerning life itself, that unavoidable haunting line: "What, oh what, does it all add up to?" On the other hand, at other times, as on this trip, I know that it has also often been the true defining and satisfying center of that life, *literature,* talking about it, wanting so much to write it, teaching it and trying to make others savor its magic, too, learn what books can tell us is to be most valued deep in the heart during our limited and ever-vanishing yet oh-so-treasured allotment of years—no doubt, at a moment such as this, if nothing else, I guess at least I do know who I am, a rush of self-identity:

Alas, for better or worse, me, *Mister* Peter indeed.

■

After the lock's buzz, I enter the dim courtyard with its glossily green palmettoes potted in oversize urns and start climbing the worn, bare wooden stairs, a full four long flights of them, to be exact. On the third landing I can already hear a soft click and diminutive, always grinning Plácida in her blue-and-white cleaning smock surely unlatching the inner door at the top-floor landing in front of the cramped nook of a reception desk there.

And, you know, climbing higher and higher, one step after another, it's somehow really extraordinary and even a rare *gift* right now just to hear that simple sound.

—*New England Review,* 2018

Je Suis Américain

A Telling Exchange during the
G. W. Bush Administration

IN TUNIS LAST SUMMER the situation was tricky. And in light of recent headlines now in 2004, a year later, I've been thinking a lot lately about what happened to me there.

Tunisia is very much a Muslim country, and this was only a few months after the U.S. tanks had rolled into Baghdad. I was very much an American, easily pegged as such, I suppose, if only because of my accent speaking French. Plus, the Red Sox baseball cap I usually wore didn't help, though it was all I had packed for headgear to ward off the strong North African sun. I had come from my home base in Austin to Tunisia for a couple of weeks to do literary research for an essay on Gustave Flaubert's nineteenth-century novel *Salammbô*, set in ancient Carthage, as well as to gather some details for fiction of my own I'm working on.

It started not long after I stepped off the Air France flight from Paris. I took a rattling bus to the downtown to look for a place to stay. On a side street, the Hôtel Omrane was a white, balconied rise that maybe was a leftover from the French colonial regime. It looked like it catered to Tunisian businessmen, and as I negotiated a price for the night with the cheery young desk clerk, he asked me where I was from. He was just making conversation, seemingly already aware of the answer because of that American-accented French from me.

"Je suis américain," I told him, then added, pretty self-conscious, "malheureusement." Translated: "I am an American, unfortunately."

In his neat blazer and tie, he got a kick out of that, laughing. He immediately turned to an older, rather elegant woman also working at the desk, probably a manager, telling her what I said, and she smiled, too. I registered, handing him my passport with the gold, spread-eagle Great Seal on the cover, and he launched into some talk about how my being an American would certainly be no problem in Tunisia, yet I assumed that was part of his courteous desk clerk's spiel. What was more important to me was how my getting the original laugh from him broke the ice. So without intending it, I had struck upon an utterance that from then on became close to a set formula for dealing with more than a few Tunisians I met, saying right off, "Je suis américain, malheureusement."

Tunisia is usually considered an open, progressive country. Apparently, that's thanks to the leadership of the late Habib Bourguiba, the president there for about thirty years, beginning with its independence from France in 1956. Bourguiba was successful in establishing the rights of women and keeping extreme Islamic fundamentalism in check. Tunis itself is a beautiful city, a fine mix of the old and new; there's a well-preserved, particularly handsome medina, the original sector of the city that has at its center a magnificent Great Mosque from the eighth century, and there are also wide modern boulevards lined with busy sidewalk cafés and plenty of white wedding-cake French colonial architecture, even a couple of sleek high-rises. Nevertheless, and progressive or not, Tunisia is, to repeat, very much a Muslim country, at one time the seat of government administration for much of Arabic North Africa.

And the big news in any Muslim country at the moment was the American occupation of Iraq. Sometimes maybe half the pages for hard news and editorials in the newspapers were devoted to it. It always seemed to be the lead story on TV news. With respect to the latter, there came a telling scenario one evening when I got back from poking around Carthage and its ruins—where Flaubert himself wandered on a flea-bitten mule in 1858, now a pleasant thirty-minute commuter-train ride from Tunis along a wide lagoon of the blue Mediterranean—and I headed over to a small, and cheap, restaurant on Rue du Caire. I had discovered the place my first week there, returning several times for the quite amazing couscous, sticking with a winner. The tables with simple plastic tablecloths were arranged in rows, and as usual the others eating there, men alone and looking like office workers in slacks and short-sleeved shirts, all sat facing the TV hung high over the front door. When the evening news clips from Iraq came on (more U.S. soldiers in big helmets and tan camouflage uniforms over bulky body armor moving around Baghdad neighborhoods on foot patrol, obviously jumpy, as the insurgent attacks of the summer of 2003 were already beginning) those men in the restaurant—every one of them, I'd say—seemed to stop eating as if programmed to do so. They stared intently at the clips that could have been something they were going to later be tested on, returning to their own meals only when the next item and other news came on.

Still, just about everybody I encountered was *so* polite about discussing the political situation with me whenever it came up. Usually after the standard smile in response to my "Je suis américain, malheureusement" line, people always wanted to assure me that they personally had nothing against Americans. Or sometimes, expressed politely, they said they had nothing against the American people, as opposed to American politicians. It was all like my initial exchange with the hotel clerk. I got it from a smiling young cop carrying an automatic rifle on routine security duty in front of a bank in the medina; he took it upon himself to approach me and welcome me to his country, telling me how many languages he spoke (Arabic, French, Italian), very proud of it. I got it from a thirty-something businessman outside of a new government building; he came up to me while I stopped, pocket notebook in hand, to jot down maybe a short story idea there on the edge of downtown. Smiling as well, he told me in French that he had suspected I was American when he first spotted me. He brushed aside my apology for my nationality as if it were but an annoying fly, proceeding to say that he'd always dreamed of going to Miami. He talked of the beach in Miami, the gorgeous girls in Miami (never underestimate the global power of American media and the lure of the fast life), concluding, "Yes, Miami, that's my kind of city!"

In short, most people appeared to be going out of their way not to make me feel uncomfortable, and I assured myself that the "Je suis américain, malheureusement" opener was a lucky discovery indeed. On the other hand, I also had the suspicion that perhaps nobody was leveling with me, that their politeness and desire to be good hosts prevented them from saying what they were really thinking. I was well aware of what I was reading in the papers, watching on TV.

But everything changed when I ended up in a full hour of conversation with—or, more so, a heated lecturing from—the guy in the government tourism office that was located in a nook in the main Tunis train station.

It was a hot late Saturday afternoon. With most of my research work done, I thought I'd make plans for a swing around the country for a few days. I wanted to go out to Kairouan toward the edge of the Sahara, often labeled "The Fourth Holiest City in Islam" and containing the tomb of an actual companion of the Prophet, then down to Sousse, recently developed as a major seaside resort. I figured I could obtain information at that tourism office in the train station. It was a cluttered single room, currently deserted of customers. Well-groomed, the husky guy on duty there had gray hair and a mustache, wore sort of Ari Onassis–style, big-frame tinted glasses. He, too, got the usual laugh out of my opening line, soon spreading out maps on a counter and piling up glossy brochures, helping me set up my itinerary. Until somewhere during that he simply stopped, looked right at me as if he had suddenly thought of something. He asked me in French, very seriously:

"You are a Democrat?"

"Yes."

He nodded.

"John Kennedy, he was a Democrat," he said.

"Of course," I said.

"John Kennedy, he was a great man, a fine president."

"Yes."

He forgot about the maps and the brochures after that. It was just the two of us alone there, the ceiling fan slowly looping above. He began opening up to me on the political situation, then really opening up some more. Within minutes he was deep into explaining to me why the invasion and any ongoing occupation of Iraq was such an assault on Muslim dignity, stressing the importance of the city of Baghdad in Islamic history. And he gave me much of that history, his fervor growing as he soon definitely became worked up about it all, his voice alternatingly sighing and thundering. What he saw as the total humiliation in Palestine was covered in detail, too. While we talked the phone started to ring, and he went to his desk in back to apparently tell whoever was calling that he would get back to them later. I didn't understand the Arabic, but I could identify the word for "American" in it, and the gist seemed to be his informing perhaps his wife or a friend that he was busy now, he was talking to an *American*. He returned to the counter, standing there again across from me, picking up where he had left off. By the end of it he was actually thumping his fist on his heart to illustrate the hurt all Muslims felt, wanting to know what Bush, what Rumsfeld, what Powell—he listed the U.S. government perpetrators by name, as if a formal order of indictment—what they were *thinking* when they embarked on this. And any judgment on Saddam Hussein himself aside, he said, did they have any idea what the repercussions in the Islamic world would be, could they be that arrogant and that naive?

"*Bush est fou, un idiot,*" I finally put in, speaking low but with conviction. No translation needed, and it felt good to say it aloud.

"Yes, he is crazy," he said in his French, calming down now, possibly embarrassed for having gotten worked up and trying to summon back his polite and easygoing tourism-office demeanor once more, "very, very crazy." Then, after a pause, he softly added: "But John Kennedy, he was a great man."

We parted with extended happy handshaking and wished each other the best of luck in everything. If the counter hadn't been between us, I suspect this guy might have hugged me hard. I headed out of the train station and into the late afternoon sunshine; the streets were packed and the little yellow taxis honked through the clogged Tunis traffic, wonderfully meandering Arabic pop music playing everywhere. Walking along, I started putting things together. I thought about what he had said concerning Kennedy, and I told myself that granting Kennedy had faults, it was no small international legacy to have your name invoked in another country over forty years after holding office, with nearly the power to soothe and heal in the course of a political diatribe. I thought more about Iraq.

And, as said, now months later I keep going back to my time in Tunisia last summer, especially what that guy in the tourism office told me.

There certainly wasn't anything new in his lecture, but how uncannily close it rang to what a lot of us here stateside asked ourselves, incredulously, almost right from the start: What could any of the principals involved have been thinking? How could they have been so absolutely misinformed, if nothing else? Because it doesn't take any covert CIA intelligence collecting or expensive think-tank research to establish a most elementary truth. It's something most any backpacking American college kid who travels around staying in youth hostels when twenty, let's say, does learn from talking with other kids from other countries, or what a middle-aged, everyday guy like me can gather in casually dealing with people in hotels and on the street during a couple of weeks in a place like Tunis. Simply and oh so obviously: This is a large, culturally complicated world indeed, and Americans are not the only people in it. And even while taking a military stand in very dangerous times like these today, the response and opinions of those other people have to be acknowledged by outsiders, have to be respected and figured into the equation ahead of time.

Maybe one of the sad byproducts of the whole tale of our involvement in Iraq is that it has created for many Americans traveling—not only me—a need to apologize for one's nationality, to be put in a position of shared guilt and genuine shame. And granting that Americans have often had a good deal to apologize for abroad, with political ugly-Americanism sometimes appearing nothing short of a standard yet quite accurate cliché by this point in history, how markedly worse it has become with this current mess.

But in the midst of an increasingly darkening situation right now, possibly the important thing is to *not* lose sight of the alternative, *never* rule it out, though such large change could be a long time coming, all right. I mean, how good it would be to someday be a traveler—doing literary research on a great writer like Flaubert or only some routine sightseeing, whatever—and able to step out of a plane anywhere on this big green-and-blue globe with a different feeling. Step out and pronounce to somebody, not in the cornball way of another jingoistic country and western song, but with the kind of quiet and even selfless belief that's admittedly so far from our national consciousness at the moment that for me just to type it here almost feels like delivering the punch line to a joke:

"*Je suis américain, avec gratitude et fierté.*"

Yes, an American—gratefully and proudly.

—*The Texas Observer*, 2004

Postscript: It's fascinating to see how the image of George W. Bush, who bungled the Iraq War, the sad and even today continuing matter of that doomed involvement, would in time pale by comparison to the image of a more recent president operating largely via self-boasting and thoroughly wacky online tweets, a man routinely ridiculed for his crassness abroad, to the point that G. W., God bless him, has not only gone on to be more or less rehabilitated in the public eye, but also regarded by some commentators as—and who knows exactly how it has happened—a wise and very respected national elder statesman.

A Desk for Borges

Reality is not always probable—or likely.

—Jorge Luis Borges

SOME YEARS AGO, when I was living and teaching in Paris on an academic exchange, I went to a dinner party. No sooner was I handed an aperitif by the host and encouraged to help myself to the decidedly complicated hors d'oeuvres, than I was introduced to one French writer there as being somebody who was a faculty member at the University of Texas—he was *extremely* impressed. Yes, he said that he did know about the institution, and he seemed to admire the very idea of the University of Texas simply because, to paraphrase his French: "Of course, that's where Borges once taught."

His response has always stuck with me. And it might be as good a place as any to start on the story of the wonderful association with the university of the Argentine literary giant Jorge Luis Borges, who did teach regular classes at the university as a visiting professor for a semester in 1960–61 and whose innovative short stories—metaphysical in intent, bravely challenging common assumptions about time and space, reality and unreality, even what literature itself is—probably changed the look of serious fiction forever.

That response from the French writer has also led me to thinking about something else. It has to do with the label (buzzword?) that lately gets tossed around quite often on this campus and others, with the whole business of the school announcing itself on many fronts—sometimes maybe too loudly in its understandable high spirits—as "world class"; it's a consideration I'll get to in a bit here, and somewhat grumblingly, too, to forewarn you.

But first for some of the facts in an amazing twentieth-century life, that of Jorge Luis Borges.

■

Born in 1899 into a historically prominent family, with an ancestry that included nineteenth-century Argentine military commanders on both sides, Borges grew up thoroughly bilingual in Buenos Aires; his grandmother was British and his father, a sometime attorney, was a great admirer of England's literature. English was so much a part of his early life that Borges later liked to note that as a boy he had first read some of the classics of Spanish literature in the English translations he found in his father's extensive library. The family moved to Europe for several years, where Borges attended Swiss schools and later became involved in avant-garde poetry circles in Spain while in his twenties. He returned with the family to Argentina and took up with like-minded young poets who were bent on shaking things up in what they saw as the stuffy Buenos Aires literary scene, publishing broadsides and refusing to docilely accept the beliefs of established luminaries.

Tall, as good looking as a tango crooner, he was shy by nature and also had the habit of falling head-over-heels for rich Buenos Aires socialites. They saw him as a good companion for talk about books, though when it came to marriage they inevitably opted for a more well-to-do prospect. Actually, it was while he was hurrying to meet a young woman for a date that he bounded up the stairs to her apartment and struck his head on an open steel window frame, suffering a gash that became badly infected; there was an operation and long hospitalization, complete with feverish delirium. Upon recovery, he was fearful that he had lost some of his faculties, and to challenge himself and test his mind, he tried writing what would be something new for him, a short story rather than a poem. The result was "Pierre Menard, Author of the *Quixote*." In the story, a dabbling contemporary writer in Nîmes, France, sets out to do more than just rewrite the Cervantes masterpiece: he wants to create it word for word exactly and as the product of his own imagination— which he does, showing how any great book maybe taps into a universal creative consciousness and has an existence of its own, independent of even the author. Borges said the story was a breakthrough for him, and in a subsequent burst of creativity that lasted a decade or so he wrote a couple dozen more short stories equally as challenging. "Death and the Compass" takes its erudite detective protagonist on a quest to solve the murder of a renowned Kabala scholar, with the sleuth's discovery that the solution apparently lies in understanding a timeless alternate dimension. "The Library of Babel" is about a strange and limitless library of hexagonal towers, where one text only leads to another, and that to another, and so on, vertiginously, for what observers today see as a prophesying of the whole seemingly unbounded universe of information that we currently call the Computer Age. The tongue-twistingly titled "Tlön, Uqbar, Orbis Tertius" tells of a secret cult that succeeds in establishing that an invented world is a real one because articles describing that land in detail—right down to an analysis of its odd language that contains no nouns—exist in a very real encyclopedia.

This was fiction that in form and content ventured well beyond not only traditional realism, which suddenly looked as passé as a backfiring Model T, but also the writing of daringly experimental practitioners such as James Joyce and Virginia Woolf, both of whom Borges admired and translated; with Borges now using the short story to examine in depth a host of intriguing matters (the meaning of philosophical paradox, the implications of mathematical infinity, etc.), narrative progressed in a single high-flying leap from the still emotional tenor of modernism to the probingly intellectual one of postmodernism. The first stories were gathered together in what would prove to be the seminal volume *Fictions* in 1944, and the collection *The Aleph* followed in 1949.

During those years, Borges lived modestly, bordering on monkishly, with his widowed mother in a Buenos Aires apartment. His eyesight had begun to fail him in mid-life, a situation that gradually worsened and led to all but total blindness. He earned a living as an assistant at a branch library in a bleak end of the city. Putting the innate shyness aside, he took political stands and became a vocal opponent of Colonel Juan Domingo Péron (Borges's elderly mother and adult sister themselves were once arrested for demonstrating against the thuggish dictator and his locally besainted wife, the former radio actress Evita Péron); he resigned from the library assistant's job when some Peronista flunkies—for a cruel joke, the way Borges saw it—tried to reassign him to another government position, as chief inspector of poultry and rabbits in the city's Calle Córdoba public marketplace. However, in a fitting and dramatic reversal of fortune once Perón was at last ousted in 1955, Borges was made director of Argentina's prestigious National Library, the equivalent of our Library of Congress. He held the post for almost twenty years.

Eventually, his writing would be translated and then loudly celebrated abroad. The very first to do so, as is often the case, were the spookily insightful French, who, it should be remembered, also rescued both Poe and Faulkner from impending oblivion. Borges was the spiritual godfather for the whole 1960–70s generation of dazzling young American experimenters in fiction—Donald Barthelme, John Barth, Robert Coover, and William Gass all acknowledged his strong influence. In fact, Borges soon became an icon for the new and culturally hip in general, and amid the blaring rock music and confusing group sex in the 1970 Mick Jagger movie *Performance,* the star is shown in one scene stretched out in a bubbly bathtub in a London flat and studiously reading a volume of, naturally, Borges. Though his most significant writing was finished before he was fifty, the last couple of decades of Borges's long life proved to be a continuing international tribute to the man and his achievement— Borges jetting all over the world, the honorary degrees and orders of merit from various governments piling up.

In 1986 he died in Switzerland. He was traveling with his longtime companion/secretary María Kodama, whom he married two months before his death, probably so she could keep control of his literary estate; she was thirty-nine and he going on eighty-seven. He's buried in Geneva, which Kodama held was his own strong wish, contending he didn't want his remains returned to his native land. Apparently, Borges was convinced Argentina had been ruined under the vicious military rule of the 1970s and 1980s, despite the fact that he himself—known for a stubborn conservative streak toward the end, once even dedicating a translation of Walt Whitman to Richard Nixon!—did publicly support, in the name of political stability, those same generals and admirals when they first took over. His stand on that came to trouble him terribly as he gradually learned of their clandestine bloody tactics, and it's usually thought that his backing them most likely kept him from being awarded the Nobel Prize in literature.

■

While Borges's time in Austin does receive some mention in the three full-length biographies of him available in English, the best and surely most heartfelt document regarding Borges and the University of Texas is a several-page memoir written by a professor in the Spanish department in the 1960s, Miguel Enguídanos; it serves as the introduction to Borges's book *Dreamtigers* and I'll borrow from it extensively here. Also, realizing that there are those on campus today who, without question, know a whole lot more about Borges's stay than I do and who even had firsthand experiences with the man, I'll nevertheless try my best to convey what I've learned through reading around some on my own and informally talking to people concerning the visit.

Under the auspices of a Tinker Visiting Professorship in Spanish, which still operates with a mandate to bring Latin American writers to the university, Borges arrived in Austin in September 1961 and, according to the schedule of the old semester calendar, was in residence right through January 1962. His mother accompanied him, and he taught two courses in Batts Hall; one was an overview of his homeland's poetry and the other a seminar on Leopoldo Lugones, a leading Argentine modernist. During the semester he also delivered open lectures on other major Argentine writers and Walt Whitman.

Actually, placing this moment in the context of his career becomes significant, because at that time the full, loud worldwide acclaim for Borges described above was yet to come, granting he was past sixty years old. I think that it stands as a testament to the caliber of the university's Spanish department of 1961 that by inviting him, the powers that be within the department exhibited respect for his work comparatively early and therefore had the admirable prescience to realize just how important that work would soon prove. As said, the French had given him his earliest recognition beyond Argentina with some translation into their language in the 1950s, and shortly before coming to the university he had been named the co-winner, along with Irish writer Samuel Beckett, of a new, but not yet very well known, achievement award backed by publishers from several countries. However, the University of Texas was the first U.S. institution to seek him out and bring him to a campus. In fact, though he did later have academic residencies elsewhere in the United States, lecturing at Harvard, Indiana University, and Michigan State (the Harvard and Indiana appointments entailed public talks, and the Michigan State teaching position was rather brief and interrupted by considerable travel), Texas was the only American university where he actually taught scheduled classes as a faculty member for an entire regular semester, which turned out to be that significant note in Borges's CV that the citizen at the dinner party in Paris remarked to me about.

Professor Enguídanos describes well the excitement that surrounded Borges's visit. It began almost as soon as his plane touched down in Austin following a rare and metaphorically apt hurricane that blew in from the Gulf Coast, delaying his arrival. Enguídanos writes: "To evoke the impression he made in the many hours he lived among us is not easy. Within a week there was talk about Borges, with Borges, because of Borges, and for Borges, in every corridor of Batts Hall. Scholars felt obliged to write studies and theses on Borges's work. Poets—wasn't it inevitable?—fired dithyrambic salvos at him." People still remember his classes to this day. Quite pleased himself to be here, his very first time in the States, and fully appreciative of the attention he was being given, he showed that the enthusiasm was a two-way street, as an ever-smiling Borges immersed himself in academic duties as well as what he found the stimulating intellectual environment overall of the comparatively small but vibrant campus town of the period. Back in Argentina Borges had recently embarked on a project to learn the Old Norse of the great Icelandic sagas, organizing a group of Buenos Aires university students to study it with him; in the person of Rudolph Willard, a professor of Old and Middle English in the University of Texas English department, Borges had found somebody who shared his interest, resulting in extended afternoon discussions on the subject in Willard's office. Before long Professor Willard became a good friend. Thomas Whitbread, still an active member of the English department today, tells of attending an evening get-together with other faculty members and Borges. Upon discovering that Whitbread's field was contemporary American poetry, Borges, the inquisitive lifelong student, only wanted to hear everything that Whitbread could tell him of Robert Frost now that he, Borges, had cornered somebody who might be an expert on the American poet who intrigued him so.

In more casual moments, Borges met with friends and students to discuss literature in the old all-night Nighthawk restaurant/diner on the main thoroughfare across from the campus, Guadalupe Street, aka "The Drag." His mother was an elegant, albeit occasionally snooty, matron, who when in Argentina never failed to remind people of her son's hallowed lineage, but she appeared to let down somewhat in her haughtiness once she was in the U.S., often accompanying Borges (whom she always called "Georgie," using the English diminutive) to social gatherings; avid moviegoers, the pair of them sat through multiple screenings of Hitchcock's *Psycho* at the Varsity Theater—Borges sight was nearly gone at this point, though he was still capable of distinguishing shapes and limited color if he took a seat up front. When he did express some homesickness for Buenos Aires, colleagues would drive him to Town Lake, where he enjoyed sitting and relaxing for a while and where the water's muddy aroma reminded him of the wide, majestic, and very muddy River Plate in his native city. All reports speak of him as being an unassuming, good-natured man, ever the bachelor librarian at heart whose whole life was basically and nobly that of books.

One of the most amusing anecdotes about his visit that I've heard told involved Borges's desire to go to San Antonio, where he would visit the Alamo and give a newspaper interview. He loved the writing of the *fin-de-siècle* British aesthete Oscar Wilde, and he had read that Wilde himself had once spent time in San Antonio during a lecture tour in America. Borges asked those in the Spanish department if they might be able to find out where Wilde had stayed, because he would like to stay there, too. Borges was assured by them that it must have been what had always been the indisputable landmark hotel in the city, the Menger. A secretary from the department called the hotel ahead of time, to ask, "Do you know if the Menger is where Oscar Wilde stayed in San Antonio?" only to be told by the desk clerk, possessor of a strong Texas twang, that he couldn't be certain, but he would get back to her. Which he did the next day, informing her, Texas twang as strong as ever, "I went through the register book for the whole past year, ma'am, and no fella by that name has ever been here—I'm sure of it."

Borges got a kick out of that, and he did stay at the Menger, right beside the Alamo, even if he didn't have confirmation of the Wilde residency.

In his busy schedule, another trip was organized out to the South Plains and Texas Tech University in Lubbock to give a lecture, and the editors of the *Texas Quarterly*—a lushly packaged literary journal with a solid national reputation that was once published at the university and later unceremoniously disposed of by the university administration in the early 1980s—put together an issue featuring a number of his poems in translation and verse honoring him by British poet Christopher Middleton of the German department. The head of the university press at the time, upon the urgings of those in the Spanish department, apparently set out on a mission to approach Borges and ask about the possibility of translation rights to any of the Borges books in Spanish for the then relatively new Texas Pan American series, devoted to important modern literature from Latin America in translation. Borges agreed to have the press bring out in the U.S. in 1964 a collection of poetry and short prose pieces, *Dreamtigers* (titled *El Hacedor* for the original 1960 Spanish edition). Jointly translated by Mildred Boyer, a Spanish professor at the university, and the poet Harold Moreland, the slim volume remains one of the most important Borges books in English today; in its pages can be found the cryptic, and iconically Borgesian, brief narrative piece called "Borges and I" on the idea of any author as not himself or herself but a ghostly Other, which has emerged for some contemporary scholars, it seems, as far more than a mere text to be analyzed and nothing short of an indispensable pronouncement in the canon of postmodern literary theory. *Dreamtigers* has gone through close to a dozen printings and is still offered by the press in the paperback edition with a distinctive cover that uses an original woodcut by the noted Uruguayan artist Antonio Frasconi, reproduced in bold black and russet on white and showing a wild-eyed tiger prowling through shafts of skewed, dagger-like jungle grass—expressionistically intense, the image is very appropriately the stuff of strange night-imaginings indeed. Mortimer J. Adler, founder and guru of the Great Books Foundation, once pronounced *Dreamtigers* a "masterpiece" of the twentieth century, and Borges himself would comment on how it held a special place in his own heart, calling it his "most personal" volume of work. I myself suspect there has never been a more significant title published by the press.

To return to Professor Eguídanos's account, the introduction to *Dreamtigers,* here's a passage that gives a moving concluding assessment of what Borges's visit meant to the university, as it sums up the rare effect he had on those with whom he came in contact:

But how can I express the accents of his voice grave and sweet, the flight of an extraordinary intelligence and imagination, the candor of a good and innocent soul, the quiet ache of a darkness and a loneliness we sensed, the magic of the poet who makes dreams come to life?

Many times I guided his uncertain steps through halls and down stairways, over the rough places of the island that is this out-of-the-way university. His poor sight allowed his friends the paradoxical task—misfortunate fortune—of guiding the best *seer* among modern writers in the Spanish language. To walk beside Borges, the great peripatetic conversationalist, was to enter and live in his world. The guide soon discovered, by the light that matters, that he himself was the blind one, and not the poet leaning on his arm.

A fine evocation of just how grateful Eguídanos himself and many others were to have spent time with him.

■

Borges never forgot his experience at the university either. The two-way street that characterized the relationship certainly didn't end when he flew back to Argentina.

In subsequent years he visited many campuses in the United States to deliver lectures and attend symposiums on his writing, yet he frequently assured people that Austin remained his favorite spot in all of America, and he returned to the university for briefer visits in 1976 and 1982. On both occasions he spoke to packed audiences, and during one stay he was taken on a freewheeling picnic with some Spanish department grad students, a lot of fun for all concerned. (I was recently told about that day by the former grad student who organized it, now middle-aged and a university professor of Spanish literature herself, as excited today about the afternoon spent with Borges as when it happened; she's the young dark-haired woman peering intently over Borges's shoulder as he signs a book in the photo on page 185 here.)

Sometimes there seemed to be no bounds to Borges's affection. He's said to have on one occasion told an interviewer that he found Austin to be the most beautiful city in America. The interviewer did respectfully challenge him on that, reminding him that he was almost completely blind at that stage, so how, in fact, could he pass judgment on the city being beautiful? To which Borges, his grin wide, reportedly provided an answer fitting of an author who was the master of metaphysical literature, somebody ever suspicious of the very concept of dominant reality: "I find it so beautiful because I *dream* well there." When the novelist Paul Theroux traveled entirely by rail from his home in Boston to Argentina and interviewed Borges there—a long, adventurous journey described in Theroux's bestselling 1979 nonfiction account *The Old Patagonian Express*—Borges asked Theroux, almost before the American writer could get through the door to Borges's book-clogged apartment in central Buenos Aires, if he had stopped in Austin on his trip. Theroux said no, and Borges chided him for having missed it and emphasized the intellectual importance of the place, an offbeat exchange wittily described by Theroux in his book.

Homage to his Texas experience turns up in Borges's work as well. In the hefty, posthumously published *Selected Poems* of Borges (1999), the editor assembled the book so that the very last poem, a place of honor, is given to "The Web," where an aging Borges speculates on which of the several cities in the world that he has appreciated in life ("my cities," as he refers to them) he might one day die in: "Austin, Texas, where my mother and I/ In the autumn of '61 discovered America?"; in another poem, "Elegy," he looks back on his past and mentions having been "part of" Texas. And there's, of course, his beautiful sonnet on the state, "Texas," where he finds haunting geographical, historical, and even mythic parallels between it and his Argentina. Often anthologized, "Texas" has been translated into English by several poets—and also wannabe poets, unfortunately, of the ilk who proceed with but an elementary knowledge of the other language and dictionary firmly in hand—yet nobody has ever come close to the sonorous and darkly lyrical version done by the Pulitzer Prize–winning contemporary poet Mark Strand (as a note, Strand's translation was once reproduced on a handsome little commemorative card printed by the university's rare books and manuscript library, the Harry Ransom Center, and lately is a collector's item). Borges even set an entire short story about some academic intrigue, "The Bribe," on the campus, with it taking place in a faculty office in Parlin Hall, home of the English department; the main character—a venerable scholar of old New England stock—appears to have been based on Borges's good friend who discussed Old Norse with him, Professor Willard.

∎

And maybe I can insert here yet another anecdote concerning Borges and the University of Texas, this one my own. It does figure in, and it might also serve as a good way to loop my way back, at long last, and approach what I started this off with—how the whole idea of Borges and the school has gotten me to thinking about what does make for a truly world-class university.

It happened just a few years ago in the creative writing course I teach every spring, English 355K: "Advanced Creative Writing." It's the final course in the sequence of undergraduate creative writing offerings, and I can honestly say it's my absolutely favorite class to teach, graduate courses included, one I always intently look forward to. E 355K tends to attract some of the very best young literary talent on campus, and the students who enroll in it are inevitably, well, outright terrific.

Because E 355K is different than mosts creative writing courses, in that it accommodates both aspiring fiction writers and poets, I assigned as a spring-break reading project that year Borges's *Dreamtigers*. With its first half devoted to short prose pieces and its second to poems, *Dreamtigers* is one of those rare literary documents that demonstrates how an exceptionally gifted writer can excel in both genres—which often seem quite dissimilar, even at odds—and how each genre can, in fact, feed the other in the overall creative process. (Besides the short stories he's best known for, Borges did produce a substantial body of poetry, much of it evoking the unique atmosphere of what can become his airy, dreamlike Buenos Aires; especially strong are the early volumes from the 1920s,

Fervor of Buenos Aires and *Moon Across the Way*). I guess another reason I assign it is because of my own longtime obsession with Borges's work and constantly wanting to spread the word on it, plus my hope that it will excite students the way it first excited and inspired me as a younger writer. (Having been away on leave in 1982, the single time Borges visited the university during my tenure at the school, I missed seeing Borges in Austin, but I did hear him deliver his Charles Eliot Norton Poetry Lectures on a succession of autumn evenings in Cambridge, Massachusetts, when I was an undergrad at Harvard in 1967, the start of my own Borges obsession. Said obsession once even led me to journey the long five thousand miles to Buenos Aires—solo and traveling with little more than a couple of changes of clothes and some Borges texts stuffed in a small suitcase—for no other reason than I wanted to reread the work *in* Buenos Aires, the place of its uncanny creation.) When assigning *Dreamtigers* before spring break, I told the students that they could respond to the experience of reading it in whatever format they wanted, but limited to about a page—a poem, a letter, or a brief reading-journal; I planned to have each read aloud his or her response to those in the class on the first day we met following the break. This particular semester campus construction meant that classrooms in the English department's Parlin Hall were often used by other departments, while English classes, in turn, got shuffled somewhere else—it had something to do with the size of rooms and the time slots needed for the meetings—and wouldn't you know it, just the year that we were reading Borges, E 355K was relocated from its regular venue of Parlin Hall to a room in Batts Hall. Better yet, Batts Hall was at the time definitely the "old" Batts Hall that Borges himself must have known when the Spanish department (then part of the Department of Romance Languages and later Spanish and Portuguese) had been located there. That meant it still had considerable character, with fine dark woodwork, lumpy yellow plaster walls, and kidney-bean red linoleum floors, before Batts, like so many other campus buildings, fell prey to more of the incessant "renovation" at the university, which does have a tendency to render even the classrooms in impressive older buildings, such as Batts there on the school's stately South Mall, clinically bland within and somehow pretty character*less*—in my opinion, anyway.

I was late getting to the class that day, hurrying from Parlin across the South Mall after the bells on the Tower had chimed three. I strode into the room on the first floor, where the big windows were shoved wide open to the balmy late-March day—blossoming and sunny and oh-so-fragrant—and I maybe muttered some apologies about having gotten tied up with a phone call back in my office, which was true. Unpacking my book bag at the teacher's desk, however, I seemed to notice something was different, though at first I wasn't sure exactly what it was. Yes, a few of the dozen or so students had acquired very good tans since I had last seen them, probably from time logged at the beach during spring break, but that wasn't it. And, yes, they had arranged the old desks with seats attached, each all one piece, in a semicircle as they always did when they first got to the room, before the start of every class; it was the configuration we regularly used for workshop discussion of the students' short stories and poems and what we would use in this class for their reading aloud their responses to *Dreamtigers*, a copy of which most of them had ready on the flat, marred desktop slabs. The book's distinctive cover with the aforementioned tiger being repeated atop the semicircle of desks made for a rather nice fan pattern from my vantage point up front, but that wasn't it either—no, that wasn't what seemed to be different this day. Sitting down at the teacher's desk, I finally realized what it was.

A single student desk—very much so one of those ubiquitous one-piece units with seat attached that were once found in just about every American schoolroom—had been placed exactly in the center of the semicircle, which *did* look weird to me, it simply being there and empty like that. But when I asked what was the deal on it, the students explained they had carefully positioned the desk that way; they said it was all intentional and also only right, the bunch of them agreeing—enthusiastically, near chorally—with something along the lines of:

"It's for *Borges!*"

You have to understand that I hadn't even lectured on Borges at this point, so whatever they knew about his work they had discovered in their own reading of *Dreamtigers* during vacation. Nevertheless, I had no doubt that with the students having come up with this wonderful idea entirely on their own, I could rest assured that I didn't need to launch into any prefacing explanatory lecture on Borges. They might have read *Dreamtigers* on a 737 flying back from their parents' home in a Dallas suburb, or by the palm trees and waves in Cancun, or just stuck in a grim West Campus apartment in Austin because they didn't have the money to get away for spring break, but wherever it had been, they had understood the underlying message of Borges's writing. It's a message that announces that those common assumptions about time and space are certainly meant to be challenged (critics often note that what Einstein did for physics, Borges did for literature), and where the validity of the dreaming world can become more significant than that of the waking one; it's a message that also suggests how art itself can indeed offer a transcendence in its shedding of the limitations of the corporeal, the thumpingly chronological, too, so that for all intents and purposes once you are taken up by a book—in this case once it is moving you into a realm of possibility and wonder with the heady power of words, as genuine literature can, and once you have subsequently assembled with fellow students in a classroom to read aloud and share one-page responses to an author's work—it makes perfect sense that the author is actually alive and right there with you.

So, just maybe a silver-haired, ever-smiling Borges, well groomed in a tailored business suit as usual and baggy eyelids half lowered in his blindness, *was* seated at that little desk in the semicircle's center that afternoon in the same building, Batts Hall, where he himself had once taught, there again to eagerly listen to these students talk about his book.

No?

■

OK, now for a bit of a shift and to move on to my larger argument.

Universities in the United States long to be internationally acclaimed today. Global recognition is the cry on many campuses. In fact, I suspect the University of Texas paid a hefty amount to an advertising firm to come up with its supposedly appealing, pretty presumptuous slogan for the school to announce such aspiration: "What Starts Here Changes the World." (As in much else lately, marketing emerges as a prime mission, and if household cleansers have always had catchy slogans and car insurance companies more recently vie with one another to have the very catchiest, why not have higher education abandon its former admirable dignity and enter the blaring promotion game, too?) At the time of this writing, many large universities also wield more wealth than ever, endowment investment compounding, despite routine complaints about cutbacks and lack of funding.

Considerable financial support for the University of Texas comes from revenues generated by leasing properties it owns in the oil-rich orange sands of West Texas, a particularly profitable source for some years due to the boom in fracking. Labeled the Permanent University Fund, much of this income goes into physical facilities as well as a rather amorphous category of system-wide "administration," though, surprisingly, only a lesser chunk is specifically designated for student financial aid, and that mainly for graduate students. Facilities being a high priority at the university, new construction never ends, as accompanied by the previously alluded to gutting and remodeling of buildings, surely generating lucrative contract deals that can result in appreciable benefit for those with statehouse and board of regents connections. This also makes for a hopefully attractive campus, which provides an advertising vehicle in itself for any school. And with its handsome Mediterranean architecture the central campus at the University of Texas *is* attractive, granting that some of the newer buildings are absolute design disasters, as architectural critics have noted, among these a campus art museum that's suggestive of a colossal, painfully glorified Walgreens. (I do remember that when I taught for a semester at the Sorbonne Nouvelle in Paris, my classes were held in a bleak concrete city building splattered with graffiti on unfashionable Rue Censier, as run down as any neglected urban housing project; but in France ideas and learning were the priorities, and the physical mattered less in comparison to the material of the mind, which is probably why the Sorbonne is, well, the *Sorbonne*.) One of the ultimate excesses—obviously nothing new, very old news—can be witnessed in the vast sums poured into athletics at universities, maybe paying a coach more than a major Wall Street CEO; instead of raising eyebrows, such indulgence provides sports-mad alumni welcome proof of how downright dedicated the school is to fielding a successful team. I saw recently that the football squad's locker room at the University of Texas was redone with some sort of state-of-the-art lockers that resemble complicated space capsules. A little online checking reveals that each has: a thirty-seven-inch television on top with a glowing full-color image of the player as the home screen; soft lighting within; individually controlled ventilation; an apparatus to dry out a sweaty helmet plus another to do the same for equally sweaty cleats; handy USB ports; a digital safe box; as well as nice little custom touches, like the team's Longhorn logo artfully set into the gleaming stainless steel glove hooks. Each unit reportedly cost just under ten thousand dollars. True, a comparatively minor instance of extravagance in the overall scheme of things but a revealing one nevertheless, akin to those ever-recurring tales of U.S. government overspending, such as the Air Force's infamous ten thousand dollar toilet seats. Also, ten thousand dollars per locker for about a hundred squad members adds up, and though I certainly do enjoy watching football and played sports myself in high school and college, I am an alleged educator, too, and one who is aware of cash-strapped families up against escalating tuition costs and graduates saddled with enormous debt, so I can't help but wonder when I read that the final total tab for the luxurious redo of the whole football locker room complex came in at a cool seven million. (Please erase all memory of your own beloved old gym locker in high school with the tinny olive-green door and click-clicking dial padlock.) In the end, the reality of the situation is that glitzy buildings, sweet deals on construction, multimillionaire coaches, and other similar excesses too long to list here most likely don't have much influence on a university's reputation beyond pleasing local boosters or a limited regional audience at best, because the bulk of it is only a matter of more of the usual—*money*.

And the situation is not just here at the University of Texas. It's close to de rigueur at a good number of institutions across the country today. Increasingly in America, education has become a competitive big business led by an upper echelon of campus administrators. They're higher-ups who are often far removed from the actual activity of instruction, more akin to a clique of wheeler-dealer corporate executives, really, which is what their jobs understandably do demand, including any major university's sky-high-salaried cadre of a president and multiple vice presidents and provosts for this and that. Meanwhile, the students—especially undergraduates—can sometimes feel almost ancillary and mere customers who must simply be kept reasonably served and acquiescent enough not to interrupt the necessary commerce and continual PR boasting about latest fund-raising figures and such (take it from a thirty-year-plus faculty member who has witnessed this situation firsthand, the odd and off-putting corporate atmosphere in academia it has generated today). To repeat, concerning an outlook and even wrongheadedness of this kind, as well-intentioned as the motives might be of those involved, usually quite able people, I tend to doubt that very much of it *changes* the world as we know it.

As opposed to this, the whole fascinating story of Borges and the University of Texas perhaps provides at least an example of one valuable paradigm that any large, established school might follow in reaching its full potential, something that never should be lost sight of. It began with a specific episode when a number of the university's resources—as elaborated above: a concerned, prescient departmental administration; energetic and outstanding faculty members from several other departments; a top-notch university press; eager, inspired students; and even the larger community of the university's city itself—they all came together with vision and solid purpose to produce something genuinely startling and with repercussions both lasting and undeniably international. I mean, don't forget the glowing image of the university that

Borges left with and then went on to tell so many others in so many places about. And don't forget either how that writer in France all but bowed to me with Gallic elegance at the dinner party, how he marveled to me about the university's excellence, just because Borges had taught there.

Talk about a proud moment, one when, for me in faraway Paris, there was no questioning of my university being world class—and then some.

■

There is nothing on campus named after Borges that I know of, though I once saw a great bumper sticker, bright red, on the door of a young assistant professor's office in the Spanish department that said, "Honk If You Love Borges!" Zulfikar Ghose—a recently retired professor in the English department and an exceptional novelist, poet, and essayist with twenty or so books authored, who, in all honesty, has been one of the maybe two or three members of the department (the *only* member?) during my time at the university who might be considered to wield a major, genuinely global and world-class reputation, or one extending beyond the inbred coterie of academia, anyway—has suggested that Borges be re-interred in Austin. You see, there has been a drive launched by devotees to Borges in Argentina to return Borges's remains from Switzerland to Buenos Aires and its stately Recoleta Cemetery, where famous Argentines are laid to rest and where a fine mausoleum does exist for the illustrious Borges family. But argument has never let up—much of it from his widow María Kodama—to keep the remains in Geneva, and some speculate that Borges traveled to Switzerland when in failing health shortly before his death in order to die and be buried outside of Argentina, which would make a clear statement on his disillusionment concerning the brutal excesses of the military regime at home. Ghose says his idea would solve the issue and locate the site of burial somewhere that Borges always loved, as well as put it geographically about midway between Switzerland and Argentina—Austin. Also, there is the poem I mentioned earlier, where Borges muses about which of "my cities" he might someday finally find himself in when it comes time to die, which adds some fuel to Ghose's reasoning.

But, it goes without saying, Borges will never be buried in Austin, and Ghose, laughing when he suggests it, is obviously only having fun with his solution to the problem of determining Borges's final resting place, a whimsical chopping of the Gordian Knot that in itself sounds, nicely so, almost like something right out of a wildly inventive Borges short story.

The acclaimed avant-garde Scottish novelist James Kelman, winner of the U.K.'s top literary honor in fiction, the Man Booker Prize, once spent an evening with me at the Dog & Duck Pub on Guadalupe Street when he was in residence at the University of Texas as a visiting creative writing professor for a semester. In the course of the two of us enjoying spirited conversation on subjects literary and maybe too many "pints" for our own good (don't worry, neither of us was driving or had classes to teach the next day), we indulged in happily fantasizing how fine it would be to have a graduate creative writing program at the University of Texas, or anywhere else, bearing the name of Borges and therefore establishing a certain tenor for the operation. Of course, the university does now have a vibrant new graduate creative writing program, awarding a master of fine arts degree. Since 1998 it has operated under the name of the American author who wrote many bestselling historical novels, some made into successful movies and network TV mini-series, and who settled in Austin in his later years. No doubt whatsoever, he was a wise, respected, and extremely generous man. He donated literally multiple millions of dollars to the university to ensure the founding of this program, for which it's only fitting that the University of Texas proudly honor him by name, even if he himself probably would have had to wholeheartedly agree, I'd say, that as a writer he wasn't to be at all confused with somebody of Borges's stature in the bigger picture of literary history. (Borges was far from being an author on the bestseller charts at any stage of his career, including when he was most celebrated; actually, all his major short stories, those acknowledged milestones of modern world literature, originally appeared in flimsily bound, nonpaying literary journals in Buenos Aires with a relatively small circulation, which offers a meaningful lesson in how Art—keep that capitalization—does work, seldom much concerned with marketplace validation and, not to put too fine a point on it once more, *money*.) You know, now that I think of it, there's not an endowed professorial chair bearing the name of Borges, but it definitely seems that it someday might be appropriate to launch a campaign to establish one in the Department of Spanish and Portuguese. On the other hand—and not to make light of this, and with emphasis on how the observation might take on a revelatory significance—if there isn't a chair, there was a *desk* for Borges in Batts Hall that sunny spring afternoon for a creative writing class, E 355K. Which is to say, there was the sheer magic of his writing, an enduring literature, and there was the way the bright, talented Texas students, nearly a half century after he first visited Austin, were so excited about it, how they were touched and enriched and possibly changed in their own insight into life itself by that work and its dizzying suggestions of other dimensions of perception, in dreams well beyond reality or elsewhere.

I like to think that for Borges such is the kind of invisible tribute—there in the ignited imaginations of those undergrads—that he would have ultimately found most suitable when it comes to this place that was so very dear to him.

—*The Texas Book Two*, 2012

Invisible Travel

*A Cycle Concerning the Creative Imagination
in Nine Parts*

Journeys—those magic caskets filled with dreamlike promises.
   —Claude Lévi-Strauss

I am in the fourth grade and sitting at my desk in the classroom at the low-slung redbrick Nausauket School in Apponaug, Rhode Island. The school is just a few streets up from a sandy beach, small, on an inlet along the rocky coastline of bluer-than-blue Narragansett Bay. It is 1956.

At the end of each day—or at least a couple of days each week in Mrs. Blaise's class and a half-hour before the final bell at three—we are told that it will be "art time." It is an announcement that is surely appreciated by the couple of dozen or so kids, but for me is maybe beyond that—for me art time is even more appreciated than being let loose for recess in the big playground with its sparse patches of grass atop the worn hard dirt there behind the public elementary school, all the squealing and running around in the salt-fresh air for tag or who knows what kind of a new game kids can invent when simply given a standard large pink rubber ball. I love to draw, and I think that it is something I do well. Other kids can sing better than I when Mrs. Marley, the classroom-roving music teacher, shows up with her pitch pipe to lead us through songs from the red-bound *American Singer* ("Old Folks at Home," "Oh! Susanna" and the like), a few of the girls with their fragile, airily melodic voices especially good at that; and other kids in my reading group called the Bluebirds can function aloud better than I with the syllables and sentences when we sit in little chairs arranged in a circle up front, granting that the Bluebirds is the most advanced group (no politically correct need to avoid blatant stratification in the 1950s, and the Bluebirds does contain the class's best readers, far above the level of those in the second-tier Robins or the very lowly Owls). Nevertheless, while many students in the class are much better at other things, I seem to be the one who is able to *draw*. Why, just the autumn before, Mrs. Blaise—plump and of French-Canadian descent, too much rouge on her cheeks and always cheery—selected me to draw a picture of the new 1956 Plymouth Savoy she'd recently bought, so she could send it to her brother, a plumber, I think, somewhere in New Hampshire. She had parked the car she was very proud of on the street outside the long row of aluminum-framed classroom windows, and for a few sessions when it again came time for drawing late in the afternoon, I would look out the windows at the stubby, stripped-down basic coupe, though afforded some measure of verve with a two-tone-paint combination, aqua and black. I would study the bulge of the chrome bumpers, the slope of the roof, the little fins toward the taillights, first sketching a pencil outline and then gradually adding some colors as chosen from the green-and-orange box of worn Crayolas, whose fragrance alone could create a pleasant intoxication. I worked away for several sessions, until I was sure I had it exactly right—the car out there on the street, with a couple of small, peak-roofed Cape Cod–style white houses in back of it and the autumn maples fiery, was now—somehow magically, even dizzyingly—on the floppy sheet before me, for all intents and purposes existing there as significantly as it did in the rumored real world. But the picture of the Plymouth, a bona fide commission you might say, is well behind me by this point in the school year, and today I do what I often do. Come art time, a student whom Mrs. Blaise has dispatched to the supply closet in the back of the classroom passes out to each of us a large fresh manila sheet, and I, anticipating, have already lifted the wooden lid and taken from the desk's brown-enameled metal bin the crayon box, once again that special waxy fragrance of it in the classroom's steam-heated warmth enough to spark a general contentment even before I do get to work on a scene that, it seems, I have often chosen to depict lately.

I don't know why, but during art time I keep drawing this one picture, over and over, of a round-top Middle Eastern building, maybe a small mosque, with a single palm tree beside it on the desert sands and a very lurid sunset above. I have no actual knowledge of where the idea originally came from, perhaps part of something that snagged in my mind from a TV show (black and white back then) or an encyclopedia illustration (usually black and white back then, too); or, most likely, it's some combination of many of those impressions that I put together in such a way that I find even more satisfying than the quiet amazement of having transported the Plymouth Savoy from the street and onto the paper, because I sense that I am now going beyond that, feel a greater satisfaction in creating something out of nothing, what possibly doesn't exist in reality but the so-rightness of it—that distant, imagined scene—makes it more significant than anything simply taken from reality.

■

We'd bring our drawings home to show our parents. And if my obsession with the one scene became what I myself tended to forget over the years, my mother would later look back in her family reminiscences, concerning various things in the past about each of us in the large family of kids, and repeatedly say to me, "You always kept drawing that one picture, do you remember that, Pete, over and over."

I answered with maybe the only answer I could give, "I suppose I do, yes, I suppose I do remember it."

When my mother died at age eighty, one of my adult sisters, by then a successful attorney who'd followed a career path similar to that of our father—a lawyer and judge—had a hard time coming to terms with my mother's passing. Being the youngest, very much so and born quite late in life to my parents, my sister and my mother spent a lot of time together when the rest of us were soon off to college and eventually lives of our own; in her sadness she asked me not long after the burial, "Where does all that goodness go when somebody dies—it can't just all disappear can it, float away as if it never had been in this world? I mean, where does it all go?"

Extremely saddened myself, I almost feel embarrassed now to say I also turned some of the mourning toward pitying myself, knowing that with my dear mother gone nobody else in the world would ever know the many things about me that my mother did, so, in a way, all such knowledge had certainly vanished as well. And, of course, nobody else would ever know that I kept drawing that *one* picture over and over—

the little mosque-like building, the desert, the palm tree, and, most of all, the overdone sunset igniting the wide, wide sky behind it.

II.

It is 1965.

At the Catholic college-preparatory boys school, a day operation, it is a Friday night and I am in the dining hall, connected by a corridor to the gymnasium where the weekly mixer dance, called a "canteen," is being held. A bunch of us, all guys, are standing around with rotund Brother Robert in his Roman collar and black robe, the cloth shiny in spots from wear and the twin cords of its braided cincture belt dangling. I am wearing a tweed sport jacket, button-down shirt, and good challis tie, maybe chinos and loafers, more or less the same as what the rest of the guys are wearing. We are in that dining hall drinking Cokes and talking, laughing some, too, and this is what often happens at these Friday night dances at the school, where girls from nearby public high schools and also the girls schools as far away as Providence (and Providence with its skyline of old art deco skyscrapers right out of *Metropolis* and the huge, nearly dreamt white marble state capitol building on its rising hill, true, Providence sometimes can seem so *far away* from our provincial campus set right in the middle of woods alternating with the cornfields and pastures of a local farm). Earlier in the evening we did what we have been looking forward to doing all week, at least make an attempt to ask some of the girls to dance, the usual rush of the smell of crème rinse in freshly washed hair, also the flattened palm of a hand actually, and near miraculously, placed on the back of a thin blouse for the slow-dancing that is just about the only thing any of us are much good at, maybe the Beatles doing "This Boy" with its patented Lennon-McCartney nasal whine; we leave the fast-dancing to the few suaver guys among us who can, in fact, successfully perform that sort of thing. If the Friday night mixer dance always wraps up at eleven and with the playing of the old standard of "Goodnight, My Love," we have well before that abandoned the low-lit gymnasium, and here in the otherwise empty dining hall we often end up like this, buying Cokes from the machine, spending time with one of the brothers from the contingent of them assigned to keep an eye on things for the dance. It's something that we are much more comfortable with than having to deal with *girls*, about whom, being at a school of this kind and surrounded by only males all week, most of us know very little, including those few select fast-dancers among us, I'd say.

Early middle-aged, Brother Robert is balding in a pattern that comes about as close as you can get to naturally providing the look of a monk's tonsure. He has a a bit of a speech impediment—probably due to the gap in his front teeth, an occasional tendency to lisp that you don't notice after a while—and though some of the other guys when among themselves have had some fun in mimicking him, I think it is all good natured enough. Brother Robert is a concerned teacher and well-liked, somebody who obviously loves the subject he teaches, world history. He manages to make it come alive, always animated in class, albeit occasionally bordering on clownish, leading us through the story of the Greeks and the Romans that fall, sometimes veering off completely on a tangent for a week or so with something not on the subject—the life of Winston Churchill who died recently, the turbulent political situation in Africa this year—whatever really interests him and that he hopes will also interest us. Bobby Larkin is there (who will be ROTC at college and lose a leg in Vietnam), and Dick Martini is there (who once pitched a perfect school-league baseball game, got married early and had kids then divorced young and died before he was fifty of a sudden heart attack, apparently having had a serious drinking problem), and Jimmy Thompson is there (a sweet guy who loved literature and was my closest friend, whose father had a job as an everyday school bus driver, Jimmy attending our school with the help of a church scholarship, and for college he would also receive scholarship offers from top-notch places like Georgetown and Notre Dame, though I never kept track of what became of him in later life). We joke around with Brother Robert, some talk about sports, some talk about various classes. In the course of it I admit to myself a deep admiration for him and most all of the brothers, something I realize even at this age. The way the school works is that there is a cooperative angle to its operation, enforced by an odd means of discipline. Each of the brothers keeps deep in the side slash pocket of his cassock-like black robe a little pad with slips that are almost like parking tickets, printed—somewhat ironically—in the upbeat green and gold school sports team colors; the slips are handed out for any kind of classroom ill behavior or even tardiness. A lower level of infraction results in a "Misdemeanor," for which the brother can check the box on the slip, and the higher, more serious level merits a full-fledged "Misconduct," a box next to it, too, with a number of boxes below each for exactly what the offense was and at the bottom a line for a parent's signature when brought home. For a Misdemeanor one has to work for an hour after school on the grounds, raking up leaves in fall, let's say, or in winter shoveling snow from the school's walkways and parking lot. It's a repeated joke we have that whenever the brothers back in their separate residence on the school campus see the weather lady on the local late-night TV news indicate on her glass chart that another blizzard is about to blow down from Canada, the word goes out among them that there will be a lot of bad behavior in class the next day, even if there isn't, to generate a lot of Misdemeanor slips in order to get the deep, boomerang-drifting accumulation completely cleared away that afternoon. The more serious Misconduct means that one shows up on Saturday morning to work for a full three hours, and the sole two times I have received one at the school I was dispatched with some other boys— who are also good students and who probably on the basis of that alone the brothers know they can trust—to work at the brothers' residence. And what I saw then somehow saddened me. I don't think I truly understood before how selfless the lives of these men are, those who day after day sit on a stool at a high desk in front of the dusty blackboard and lead us through the lyricism of Shelley and Keats or the abstract movements of the mathematical mind with the exponents and planes and parabolas of geometry and trigonometry. In the case of Brother Robert the subject is indeed the history of the dreamily distant larger world (all those little bright-colored puzzle pieces of countries on the old desk globe that one of my older sisters got for her tenth birthday, and how we as kids in the family would spend hours in the den just spinning the rattling thing on its titled axis with eyes scrunched shut and putting a finger out to make it stop and to see where or where, in fact, we had landed—the jungles of South America, the deserts of Africa, the crowded capitals of Europe, the endless blue of the endless oceans and seas—such a roulette-wheel randomness to the whole routine, mere chance and an early lesson in the way life itself worked), yes, a large world that Brother Robert was educating us in the history of, good Brother Robert. And when working at the brothers' residence, I would take out the galvanized trash cans from the stark kitchen and see the remnants of the simple fare they survived on. I would push the dust mop along the halls and past the open doors of the little white-walled cubicles, each with a single bed and a cross above it, to maybe most heartbreakingly notice the one or two personal possessions they'd brought with them from the previous life before they entered the order's novitiate when not much older than us—a pair of scuffed and very dated white bucks on the floor beside the bed, or an old well-oiled first baseman's mitt wrapped around a dirty horsehide ball on the single small bookcase provided in each cubicle—and embarked on another life altogether, entirely selfless.

The round clock on the wall in the dining hall where we have gathered is a functional office-style one, electric with bold black numerals, a red minute hand looping around and around. The clock now indicates it is nearly eleven and the dance is ending, as we finish the syrupy Cokes and Brother Robert (who knows what became of him, and so many left the religious order in the free-spirited later 1960s, who knows if he is even alive), he says to us—all in his world history class, his cheeks rosy, his lisp admittedly noticeable—"Byzantium, Constantinople, Istanbul." Which really doesn't make any sense to us. For him it's probably a preview of Monday's class, a pronouncement he most likely hopes will pique our interest. He repeats it, grinning his gap-toothed grin, with the unstated promise that we will find out all about it in class soon enough on Monday: "Byzantium, Constantinople, Istanbul, boys."

I've always remembered that.

III.

In my reading recently I came upon this line, from the French anthropologist Lévi-Strauss:

"Journeys—those magic caskets filled with dreamlike promises."

I copied it down, my fingers clicking away on the keys of my Mac-Book Pro computer, to add it to a file I keep of good quotes I come across while reading.

I stare at it even as I write it again now, here on the white screen of the Word page bordered by its royal blue, and try to figure out why it haunts me so. There is something about travel in the word "journeys," and there is something about death in the word "caskets," and there is, very hauntingly, something about the airy substance of what is commonly called life in the word "dreamlike," especially when life for me lately, now considerably older, seems unsettling, as I frequently suspect that perhaps I have made a major mistake in the course of it, devoted altogether too much time to writing fiction—my short stories and novels and the imagined scenarios within—at the expense of so much else, the real; true, there is something about the insubstantiality of it all in the word "dreamlike" in the quote.

I keep staring at the quote.

IV.

I look at the quote some more, the computer screen glowing here in Austin, Texas, where I have lived and taught creative writing classes at the university for over thirty years. I repeat the line to myself, feeling that it's like a nail puzzle, two shiny chrome-plated, flat-headed nails convolutedly hooked together, which you twist this way and that, gaze at and analyze, twist this way and that some more, until the entanglement in your hands might at last come undone, easily and unexpectedly, as softly and maybe revealingly as shed rose petals—and imagined rose petals at that—for me to realize at last something *large*, something I really should *know* in life.

But staring at the quote now, thinking about it, I don't quite make the mind-jump, grasp the message, as close as I do come to it, and the words that in turn render the phrasing of the Lévi-Strauss quoted line on the computer screen simply remain there before me, just words:

"Journeys—those magic caskets filled with dreamlike promises."

V.

According to the English honors track at college, during the last year of study one is individually assigned to a tutor to oversee an undergraduate thesis. However, before that, in the second year and third year, there is so-called Sophomore Tutorial then Junior Tutorial. These are group sessions where several students meet once a week with an instructor and together concentrate on a single author, all of the writer's oeuvre and locating it in a larger literary tradition. It seems Harvard adopted this tutorial system from the British universities, Oxford and Cambridge, and for my Sophomore Tutorial the author is William Butler Yeats.

It is 1967.

So once a week I leave the suite of rooms in Quincy House along with another English major, a lanky, wise-cracking guy named Paul, who lives with his roommates in the suite next door. And this particular winter afternoon we start out along the crisscrossing, snow-shoveled walks. We weave our way through the quadrangles of the various Harvard Houses, the two of us bundled up in the cold, both with hats and a topcoat for him and parka for me, as worn over the standard suit-jacket-and-tie attire (required for all meals, even breakfast, in the dining halls at all-male undergraduate Harvard back then, so most everybody dresses that way throughout the day for classes); we continue past the busy, traffic-filled Square and then start up long Mount Auburn Street, heading to the apartment in a gray three-decker where our tutor lives.

Our tutor recently finished her PhD at Harvard, and her husband is an instructor in the Government department. Their apartment off Mount Auburn has the comfortable simplicity typical of a young scholarly couple's place (a few items of mismatching furniture, some throw rugs—a bright Mexican-blanket pattern—on the otherwise bare, honey-varnished floors, and the walls overflowing with books); the half-dozen of us are assembled in the front room, including a slight, dark-haired Radcliffe girl, lovely, shy, and very brilliant, who wears—rather out of character, it seems—a mini skirt and go-go boots along with a prim pink cable-knit cardigan over a cotton turtleneck, the only female. Despite her saying little, everybody always listens intently whenever she has something to contribute to our discussion analyzing the Irish poet's work, the hardbound Macmillan *Collected Poems* edition open on each lap. The talk is led by our also somewhat fragile tutor, soft-voiced, who sits in a wing-back chair in the bay window of the three-decker; she is a bit indistinct there with the winter sunlight bright behind her and her long, loosely arranged hair golden, even incandescent, it seems. Toward the end of the session we share with the others our topic ideas for the major project of the semester, the Sophomore Essay, and then we mingle with one another as we take turns sitting with our tutor for a one-on-one talk to discuss individual progress—what reading we are doing for the essay and the status of work underway on a draft. My topic is not all that original, and it's true that as a sophomore in college I am not much of a budding literary scholar. Already I am far more interested in taking creative writing classes, designated by not merely numbers but, for me, almost magical letters in the university's thick course catalog—"English C" and "English N" and "English S"—admission to them determined by manuscript submission and not even counted toward the major and usually becoming an extra fifth class in a four-class schedule; I will go on to possibly hold some kind of Harvard record at the time for the number of them taken. I tell the tutor that my paper will involve, basically, Yeats's two great thematically related poems from his later stage of life, "Sailing to Byzantium," written in 1926, and "Byzantium," written in 1930. The

THE WORLD IS A BOOK, INDEED

first is a song of approach and longing, the second a song of arrival and, surprisingly in old age, the enhancement of that artistic longing, which I try to explain to her, even if I am a twenty-year-old who knows little or nothing about the very concept of old age and how an old man could be, as Yeats famously pronounces, "but a paltry thing, a tattered coat upon a stick." My ideas are indeed basic. Hearing them, the tutor politely nods, and I think she has long since come to accept that it will not be an eventual PhD and a career of literary scholarship for me. All my essays so far have been simplistically obvious and even hokey, one comparing the transcendence of the British Romantics to that found in the lyrics of Bob Dylan's "Mr. Tambourine Man," another on my firm belief in the survival of literature and the written word over the movies, very hokily titled "Pegasus and the Lion" (Pegasus, the mythological figure representing literature and poetic inspiration, and "Lion," as in the MGM lion). Most in the group are better suited to this, especially the brilliant Radcliffe girl, who in the tutorial session is addressed as "Miss Hatch," more than once dazzling the group with her whisperingly expressed meticulous research and keen scholarly insight. (I didn't know her at all on campus outside of those Wednesday afternoon sessions in the gray clapboard three-decker, but a few years after graduation it really threw me when I saw her name listed in the obituaries of the glossy alumni magazine, far in back of the issue and once you got by the tiresomely upbeat feature articles and the ads for many luxury items—good scotch and gleaming BMWs, the things slick ad men in their cluelessness must picture all Harvard grads eager to buy; in the obituary's fine print—or as I seem to remember the details—there was talk of her lifelong struggle with a chronic illness, something none of us were aware of at the time and which, it noted, brought her back to maybe California where she was from and where she died in her twenties, only her parents and siblings listed as survivors.) The tutorial session over and darkness having already fallen outside, we all tug on our heavy coats, and with my buddy Paul I head back along Mount Auburn Street. Gusting winter wind blows strong down the street now, there is an ammonia-sharp tinge to the cold air, a sure sign that more snow is on the way; we joke about how it's a good thing that skinny Miss Hatch, as very lovely as she is, isn't out here or she might literally get blown away. When a hulking, orange-and-white MBTA trolley bus passes us, the electric rod atop it suddenly emitting an extended flash of startling blue on the overhead wires, Paul in his topcoat and authentic wide-brim fedora repeats the old gag line he has used before there on Mount Auburn Street during the walks back from our tutor's apartment; cowering some, he puts on a histrionically deep biblical voice and shields his eyes with one free hand, the other holding his green rubberized book bag: "I've seen the Light!"

I give a perfunctory laugh, but I am already thinking about my paper on the Yeats poems, buckling down to do more work on it that evening.

■

In the little maize-walled dorm bedroom, I sit before the Hermes manual typewriter, a dented aluminum contraption that's set atop a copy of the *Harvard Crimson* newspaper for cushioning on the old oaken desk.

Outside the twelve-pane dormer window on this top floor of red-brick Quincy House it is snowing. (It's a place I go back to often in my mind, that suite of rooms in Quincy where I pored over the *Norton Anthology of English Literature* for hours on end, wrote paper after paper for a seminar or lecture class there.) Now and then the old silver radiator clanks loudly, then the noise trails off in a long hiss and diminishing staccato, until everything is perfectly silent again. My three roommates are gone, probably off to study elsewhere. When the phone in the adjoining sitting room rings there on the little coffee table in front of the secondhand sofa, sagging and garish maroon (we bought it from the boozingly affable House custodian Louis, who surely has repeatedly salvaged the behemoth from past students' rooms and then repeatedly resold it over the years), I let it ring and rattlingly ring. I tell myself that if it's for one of my three roommates, the call will just mean my taking a message, so it might be better to let whoever it is try back later. And usually the only person who calls me in the evening during the week is my girlfriend out at Wellesley College. No doubt about it, I am crazy about her—honey-haired, willowy, and tall, so pretty; her perfectly round steel-rimmed glasses can sometimes magnify her blue eyes to make them look giant-size, almost weird like a Martian's yet also in a such a very pretty way, if that makes any sense. And I always like the long phone sessions with her and the meandering chat about anything. Our relaxed conversations during the week can sometimes go on for an hour, each missing the other so, we say, plus considerable talk about books and art (she knows an awful lot about painting, has opened up my own world to the wonders of the Italian Renaissance and even French Postimpressionism, two of her favorite periods) or simply talk of what we have planned for the upcoming weekend when we will see each other again, *at last.* But I won't answer the phone, and I know I shouldn't take a break. Ever since the tutorial session earlier that afternoon I have been excited about writing this paper, the idea of Yeats in the sequence of his two poems first setting out for Byzantium—the golden kingdom of it by the sea, its "drowsy Emperor" and "the holy fire, perne in a gyre"—and then actually arriving there.

However, according to what I just read in the Yeats biography checked out of the undergraduate library, a sizable tome by Richard Ellman now set on the desk beside the typewriter, Yeats himself in his lifetime, of course, never did travel anywhere near that part of the world, which is something, a detail, I definitely like—his never having been there in reality but without question having more than been there in the poem.

I start typing again, continuing with the essay. The snow keeps falling, and I keep typing some more.

VI.

Journeys—those magic caskets filled with dreamlike promises.

VII.

I am having lunch with the young woman named Ilksen who has translated one of my books into Turkish. This is in Karaköy, a section of what's
known as the European Quarter in Istanbul. It is 2013, late autumn, and
quite sunny and oddly warm for this time of the year, I'm told.

The lunch is wonderful. Up on a raised terrace, the restaurant is
an open-air affair that juts out from the city's sleek, industrial-looking
modern art museum, recently converted from a former maritime warehouse, and our table is right beside the wide, blue Strait of Bosphorus.
Passenger ferries crisscross the water, gulls squealing overhead; the un-
dulating green hills and clusters of whitewashed houses of Asia itself
lay across the way. We order the spicy seafood stew she recommended,
ungarnished except for a baguette of warm, freshly aromatic French
bread, and we talk more about the book. She not only seems to understand entirely what I am trying to do in my admittedly offbeat fiction
(it is a collection of short stories she's translated, which appeared in the
U.S. several years before, with some good reviews though not much in
the line of sales), but she's also immediately engaging and a lot of fun,
the two of us repeatedly laughing together at something said.

Coming to Istanbul for a couple of weeks was spur of the moment.
I had a semester off from teaching, thanks to yet another appreciated
university grant to work on my fiction (universities, despite my frequent
complaints about certain questionable aspects of their operation, have
been the life support of my writing career); I was planning to spend
some of that time in Paris, anyway, just a few hours by jet from Istanbul,
so a visit to Turkey could easily be worked into the trip. The publisher
and I agreed that it would be good for publicity to have me visit when
the book was issued in translation, though, in truth, now that I am here
the book still hasn't been released; a third supposedly firm publication
date has come and gone. Actually, there has been a long series of delays
and postponements regarding the project, which became more understandable after my meeting with the publisher and his staff in Istanbul.
All of them bright, wide-eyed young people who undoubtedly love se-

rious and even daring literature of the innovative kind, they are maybe a little too young and wide-eyed, seemingly short on practical business sense, their enterprise obviously suffering serious cash-flow problems. I haven't had much of my work previously translated anywhere (only a couple of stories into Spanish and Portuguese, to be honest), and this isn't any regular occurrence for me, my being anything but a recognized, world-lit type of author routinely jetting to other countries to talk about my writing. Still, in this case I received an email more than out of the proverbial blue one afternoon back in Austin saying the publishing house wished to acquire translation rights, and following some friendly back-and-forthing in a few more emails concerning terms, a contract was promptly signed. Then the slowdown began. At this point—after the meeting with the publisher a couple of days before, my detecting then his own business naiveté, a young guy in over his head with projects and having a lot to learn in life—I wonder if the book will ever appear. Which doesn't bother me too much, because I am glad just to be in Istanbul. During my stay I have been avoiding, at least for the time being, the crowds of foreigners at the big-ticket tourist attractions clustered together in the historic Sultanahmet district, such as the opulent Topkapi Palace of the Ottoman sultans with its notorious Harem Quarters and the imposingly massive rise of the Hagia Sofia mosque beside it, originally built as a church in the sixth century by Roman Emperor Justinian, who ruled his storied empire from Constantinople. I've made a quick pass or two through the Grand Bazaar, but I know I need more time to explore its endless maze of stalls and shadowy aisles right out of *One Thousand and One Nights*. I assure myself that I will properly take in all the sights before I leave, and meanwhile I have set out every day from my small, family-run hotel called The Peninsula, by the sea there in Sultanahmet, and wandered for hours through the various lesser-known neighborhoods of the sprawling, always fascinating city. No, I am not really disappointed whatsoever about what seems to have happened with the translation, if only because, as said, the project has brought me here to a place where simply the idea of it has thoroughly intrigued me ever since I was young, now getting to see it for myself at last (*there* is something about long-ago Rhode Island, a smiling religious-order brother in his black robe repeating the words that made for almost a litany regarding the thumpingly incessant and fully overwhelming progression of history, an echoing paean to the power of time and inevitable large historical change: "Byzantium, Constantinople, Istanbul"); without question, the city is proving to be everything I expected, even more.

The translator Ilksen is not so accepting of the publisher's multiple delays. Before I came to Istanbul she sent me a long email. She said how she'd spent over a year of her life on the translation, and she did so in circumstances that meant she had to sacrifice a good deal. It was time she should have been spending with her three-year-old autistic daughter, whom she often put in front of a television while she worked away, the two of them living in a small two-room flat. She had delivered the completed translation to the publisher a year earlier, exactly on time, had done the proofreading and correcting herself at the publisher's request. While she hadn't worked for this publisher before, she explained in the email that she accepted the job to begin with only because she wanted to embark on a translation assignment that truly interested her at last: "I love your work, I think I have seen through your brain cells working, I was *there*"—welcome praise, all right, but a spookily frightening proposition for me, considering that I myself seldom know if I have any chance whatsoever of seeing through my brain cells, well, *working*. But toward the end, her email turned angry, Ilksen quite heated up, as she went on to say that her initial optimism soon gave way to utter frustration with the publisher and his cockily cavalier attitude; not yet having paid her anything, he recently appeared to be dodging her completely:

"Unfortunately, there are no reply to my emails, nor to my calls. Seems like our work is tumbling in the oblivion. . . . Now that he doesn't answer my calls, I want to tear off his throat with my teeth."

I did find that comical, and understandably strange, too, so I didn't know what to expect when I met her this morning at eleven. The agreed-on spot was Taksim Square and the vainglorious bronze group sculpture of the founder of modern Turkey, the nationally revered Mustafa

Kehmal Atatürk, gazing out on the city as surrounded by an entourage of his fellow 1922 revolutionaries; they bucked the dividing-up of the country by Europeans after World War I and eventually called for abolishment of the Ottoman royal line, which in the final century of rule by the increasingly self-indulgent sultans had fallen into both personal decadence and complete administrative torpor. Any preconceptions I might have had after that email evanesced as soon as I saw approaching me in the sunshine a smiling young woman with short-cut auburn hair, walking with almost a girlish skip. She wore a coordinated autumn outfit of muted browns and oranges that could have been right out of a spread in an American women's magazine featuring what's new in back-to-campus fashion—a tweed skirt and striped wool stockings, a sort of Tyrolean jacket over a sweater, and, perfectly, a little peaked tweed cap, her animated, melodic voice itself matching the general high spirits the coordinated attire suggested.

As we talk now at the restaurant, the waiter in his black trousers and very proper white shirt comes by to ask if we would like anything else. We assure him the seafood stew was excellent, and Ilksen tells him in Turkish that we will have a coffee for me and a tea for her. With the discussion of my book and her many questions about my writing out of the way, we have comfortably slipped into talking of larger matters in life. I explain how I never married, not wishing to be tied down and well beyond doing anything permanent on that front at this stage, and she speaks more about how she went through a couple of years of total hopelessness, her only child being diagnosed with autism and at about the same time her husband suffering a stroke while not even forty. Her life collapsed around her, she says, until she just stepped back from everything, told herself that she had two choices—either wallow in self-pity or take control the best she could of the situation and decide to get organized, do something about it. I tell her that in America we would say, "You now have a game plan."

"That is it exactly!" she says. "Yes, I get for myself a game plan!"

She says that she has recently moved here from Ankara because she had pursued any lead she could on how she might help her daughter. There was a nationwide lottery for openings in a new education program in Istanbul for autistic children, an experimental school jointly run by the Turkish government and researchers from Princeton University. She entered the child's name, said a prayer to the universal deity she subscribes to—basically the benevolence of the universe hovering somewhere above us, which is what she wants to believe all religion essentially amounts to, including the Islam in which she was nominally raised in Ankara—and her daughter won a spot, half miraculously, but also half because she, hopeful Ilksen, knew it simply *had* to happen. She packed up everything and came to Istanbul, where she rents the cramped inexpensive flat and where her daughter attends the school.

Her husband is back to work at his post in Ankara, she explains, a position with a Turkish government agency, but now assigned to a desk job rather than a field one due to his disability from the stroke; he comes to visit them once a month. Her daughter is making amazing progress and is almost proving to be a prodigy, in a way, startling the teachers with her perception of colors and a rapid development in her understanding of language and numbers as well. When she speaks of her daughter, smiling, it is with such an intensity of motherly love.

The waiter brings the coffee and the tea.

Low waves lap against the seawall below the restaurant's raised terrace, the ferries out there on the Bosphorus continue to crisscross the blue water (*motherly love, and where does all the goodness go, oh, where does all the goodness go?*); atop Seraglio Point, its wooded cliff jutting up Gibraltar-like, the delicate silhouette of Topkapi Palace is visible in the distance (*a poet once dreamed of sailing to Byzantium, he refused to believe that an aged man is but a paltry thing, because there may be something beyond and even trumping that, a visionary golden empire of the creative imagination indeed*). And as we sit there at the restaurant and talk some more, the entire scene is softened by a thin, sun-charged haze on this warm and sea-fragrant November day.

I say to her:

"So the game plan is working."

She appears excited about just the thought of that, confirming it to herself and saying in her jangling, musical voice:

"Yes, and you are right, Peter, the game plan, it works well now."

VIII.

I am walking alone.

I think it is still 2013, after I have parted with the translator Ilksen at the Karaköy streetcar platform.

We leisurely strolled some together after lunch. Eventually she headed off on a streetcar to pick up her autistic daughter at the child's school, and I said that I thought I might walk around for a while, gradually work my way across the long Galata Bridge and to my hotel on the other side of the Golden Horn in Sultanahmet.

The old Galata neighborhood is a nest of shops along cramped streets steeply sloping down toward the harbor. I sit for a while on a bench in the small circular park that surrounds the conical stone Galata Tower there, constructed in Medieval times by the Genoese; once merchant traders with impressively far-ranging influence, they managed to control and oversee this sector of the city for two centuries. It's a good spot to rest for a bit and make some notes, and I tug off my fleece jacket—the afternoon is so warm—and begin doing just that. The notebook is of the sort I've celebrated in my writing often—I swear by them. It has a black marbleized cover and looks like a miniature "composition book," or a small parody of the usual larger ones, and I've already filled several such notebooks on this trip. They come in packs of four at the dollar store in Austin, the covers green or blue or red or black; the color-coding makes it easy to keep them in order, and throughout the trip I have been scribbling notes on what I have been experiencing here in Istanbul in all my walking, in all my meeting with people as well. Sometimes my notes are just random observations that come to mind—how so many people in Istanbul seem to be wearing expensive New Balance running shoes with the oversize *N* on the side, but when I looked at a pile of them in a sales stall while finally spending more time in the massive arcade of the Grand Bazaar the other day, I saw they are all cheap Chinese knock-offs; or how on the television evening news that I watch at the small hotel, there appears to be a set policy among the stations to devote a major bulk of the coverage to the current head of state, Recep Tayyip Erdoğan, probably an enforced government code and always with the intent of attempting to make the scraggly, rather nondescript man look *very* statesmanlike while speaking at any number of staged events, this despite the fact that his former glowing image in the West as a progressive has been irreparably damaged by his dispatching brutal police in riot gear, powerful water-cannon trucks backing them up, to violently quell the street protests in Gezi Park up by Taksim Square the summer before—yes, sometimes the notes are random, but sometimes they are more calculated and with ideas for short stories set in Istanbul that keep coming to me while I explore the city—characters I might use in them, sequences in the narratives beginning to build in my mind even if they maybe never will actually build on the page. When a pack of high school kids in uniforms go squealing by—young and happy, pigeons scattering in the splashed sunshine before them; classes must have just let out for the day—I glance up, then go back to the notes. I am trying to get down as much as possible of the dialogue that transpired between Ilksen and me at the museum restaurant (*as a kid sitting at my grade-school desk I looked out the window to see Mrs. Blaise's Plymouth Savoy, then looked at the finished drawing on the manila sheet before me, satisfied that what was there was now here*), and I suspect already that I might use our talk in an essay like the one you are currently reading.

After a half-hour or so, it's turning cooler. There's the sound of atonal ships' horns from the harbor below, a pleasantly nautical music, and a tour group has arrived at the little park, a guide fussily gathering them around him so he can begin his lecture on the history of the tower. I stand, slip the notebook and Bic into my back pocket, pick up the jacket from the bench and pull it on.

I start down the steep stone steps leading back toward the Galata Bridge and Sultanahmet. At one time a pontoon bridge to allow for tides, it now rests on permanent supports, and the frilled blue iron railings make for a series of—most appropriately—ornate arabesques; bell-clanking, red-and-white trolleys rattle on tracks right down the center of the bridge, the fishermen all along the railings who rent long poles adjust their their many silvery lines dangling. I suppose that with my stay here coming to a close, I am already projecting where I will be this time next week, in Paris. I will see the close friends I have there from my few times teaching on exchange at Paris universities, and I know there will be, as always, much good talk about books and authors with those friends.

By the Eminönü ferry docks, there's a buildup of heavy traffic where two wide city streets merge at an angle. I soon concede that to attempt to cross certainly isn't wise at this time of day, rush hour. Yellow taxis and grumbling, soot-spewing trucks clog the lanes, and to venture any farther into that as a pedestrian could be risky, even futile. So when I spot a nearby set of old iron stairs for an overhead walkway to the other side, I head that way and start climbing, somewhat worn out, under-standably, at end of what has been a very long day for me.

The walkway arches high above the stalled traffic. I'm the only one crossing who stops and takes everything in from the lofty vantage point—and what a show there is to take in. Out on the calm, flat Sea of Marmara scattered freighters are anchored and waiting to enter the harbor, completely motionless, almost as if dozing. The sun is setting, and it ignites the big autumn sky there above the central dome and six slim minarets of Istanbul's handsome Blue Mosque in Sultanahmet in shades that maybe can only be described by the sort of colors that are usually altogether too much to use in any writing, enough to invite valid charges of patent indulgence, especially when it comes to the matter of a sunset; nevertheless, in this case they do seem justified—melon and lavender and a rich, very brilliant vermilion, let's say.

And it is then I realize that here in Istanbul, where I somehow am at the moment (*am I here?*), I as an older man have unexpectedly stumbled onto the very scene I often drew as a child (*there might not be the desert and the shaggy palm tree, but the fact that perhaps I have at last found in reality the essential subject of the picture seems true, the sunset above a domed mosque in the East*), and I remember that my mother and I were the only people in the world who would ever have the knowledge of my drawing the one picture over and over; but that is OK, because she is very much in my mind now, alive as ever, her gentle laughter, her unflagging hopes for us children in the family; she had been a school librarian before marriage to my father, a young attorney just starting out on his practice as well as a political career then in the Depression and a true believer in Roosevelt and his New Deal, she instilled in all of us children early on a love of books and reading, an excitement about words, and it is a gift for which I have always been deeply grateful, I tell myself again even now in Istanbul as I think of her (*am I actually here, I mean, am I? are any of us actually here in this life or anywhere else? is there any chance of ever getting anywhere near the whole idea of our being alive yet given so little time on this sweet planet to savor the veritable and airily continuing wonder it ceaselessly serves up?*). I look down at the thick, stop-and-go traffic below, knowing I was wise to have used the walkway, and descend the rusted iron stairs on the other side.

■

Walking, I think more about my mother, my father, too.

And I think of French friends in Paris. Claude, the retired Saul Bellow scholar married to the beautiful opera singer Lisa and an intellectual figure as dashing, and a little crazy, as any character right out of a Saul Bellow novel; and Vanessa, undeniably brilliant, a literature professor at prestigious École Normale Supérieure and already a full professor— a level in academia that's rare and tough as all hell to achieve in France— while still only in her thirties, who a couple of years back lent me her Vélib' bicycle-share card during the summer when I lived and wrote in Paris, taking long rides throughout the city on those bikes in such sultry July and August evenings; and the other Claude, younger, a Stephen Crane scholar and his gracious wife Laure, a concerned social worker, they're raising two happy little kids in the ramshackle neighborhood where they've bought an apartment to fix up in the far reaches of the

Eighteenth Arrondissement, atop a fast-food place for halal fried chicken, no less, boom boxes blaring French rap music in that always vibrant African quarter of Paris—because, yes, this time next week I *will* be in Paris again, and, as I assure myself now, how lucky I am to have good friends like that for such enjoyable literary conversation in another country.

I pass the red-brick Sirkeci train station—once the elegant terminus for the legendary Orient Express and lately more or less abandoned, undergoing an extensive rehab project after a recent fire—and eventually I am back in Sultanahmet, where the little yellow Hotel Peninsula sits on a short, lumpily cobbled dead-end street. I think that maybe I will buy a beer and a bag of those good seasoned peanuts at the small corner store there, to take to my room in the hotel and relax with while doing some reading before dinner, an Orhan Pamuk book. I didn't have much luck with the pile of Pamuk's novels I checked out of the library before the trip—intriguing themes and philosophical concepts but the narration slow-going and never making the ultimate metaphysical leaps their premises initially promise, the writing sometimes uneven and overall lacking much depth in characterization, particularly evident when it comes to women—but I have brought with me a copy of his book of reminiscences about growing up in Istanbul. (And I might not be alone in my response, I know. Nobel Prize winner Pamuk could have been the last thing both the young publisher and the translator Ilksen wanted to talk about when I met with them; each asked me almost as soon as we first shook hands to please *not* start discussing Pamuk's work. They both said they were growing tired of the constant mention of the writer and foreigners' fascination with him, and each frankly confirmed that there might even be an unofficial consensus among literati in Turkey that not only have there been other Turks in the past more suitable for this highest international literary award—most notably the socially committed and powerfully lyrical world-class poet Nâzim Hikmet, who, after political imprisonment in Turkey for sixteen years, died in exile in the old USSR in 1963—but also, for Ilksen and the publisher, Pamuk might be but a routinely able talent from a moneyed, economically privileged class, somebody with well-honed promotional skills and serving up somewhat predictable fare aimed specifically at the tastes of a Western audience of *The New Yorker* magazine middlebrow variety, Nobel Laureate or not. But such criticism aside, I did pack in my small suitcase a paperback copy of the book about growing up in Istanbul, *Istanbul: Memories and the City,* a meanderingly meditative document in the form of a series of brief, several-page personal essays interspersed with vintage photos, and I do, in fact, find the essays entirely engaging and a valuable introduction to Istanbul, really solid, admirable work). And walking along, I tell myself that I will read some more from the Pamuk memoir once back at the hotel.

Akbiyik Caddesi is a narrow pedestrian street and the main thorough-fare in ancient Sultanahmet. Entering it, I try to look straight ahead as I pass the many absurdly overpriced and not very good restaurants, where the smarmy sidewalk touts are already trying hard to lure into them the packs of dazed tourists—mostly German and British in this off-season—until I do see the lit Efes beer sign glowing blue and white in front of the little corner store.

The first time I went there to buy an end-of-the-day beer to sip while stretched out on the bed and doing some reading at the hotel before dinner, the friendly guy at the counter asked me with the scant English he had where in America I was from. Obviously recognizing me as an American right off, he was just curious, I knew, and fortunately on this trip there has been no need for me to explain, or attempt to vocally defend, my nationality, as has happened during other travel in Muslim countries. I automatically answered "Texas." I don't often say that, never having felt genuinely at home in over three decades of residence in the state, where I've ended up living that long only because of my job. Usually I respond to such a question with "Boston" or "Massachusetts," aware that seldom if ever does anybody abroad even know where small Rhode Island is.

Stocky, mustached, wearing a sweater and jeans, the guy nodded. He put my tall can of Efes beer into a plastic sack and spoke the word aloud himself, grinning toothily wide beneath the mustache, as if he relished the sound of it: "Texas." He paused, next made a pistol gesture with his hand, forefinger out for a barrel and thumb upright for the cocked hammer on a six-shooter. "Texas cowboy," he then said, looking right at me, still nodding. In the couple of times I've been back since that day he remembers me, does the same thing, the pantomime of the quick-drawn pistol pointed at me along with the wide white grin and the slow pronouncement: "Texas cowboy."

I wonder if he will do it again this evening when I enter.

IX.

Then I get a little scared to think that maybe the mustached guy wearing jeans and a bulky sweater in a cubbyhole corner market in faraway Istanbul never did do that, the odd pantomime, and maybe I have imagined or only *dreamt* he did it.

And, you know, here in Istanbul right now I decide that I like that idea, not being sure which it was, dream or reality, and it's sort of what has happened to me an awful lot, repeatedly, in a long life of near incessant travel—which is to say *journeying,* as Lévi-Strauss would have it— where I constantly am beyond amazed by the dazzling and appreciated ongoing marvel of it all.

—*The Literary Review,* 2015

9 780807 173961